DANCE THERAPY AND DEPTH PSYCHOLOGY

As a psychotherapeutic technique dance/movement as active imagination was originated by Carl Gustav Jung in 1916. It was later developed in the 1960s by dance therapy pioneer Mary Whitehouse. Today it is an approach to dance therapy as well as a form of active imagination in analysis.

Joan Chodorow, leading dance therapist and Jungian analyst, provides a detailed exploration of the origins, theory and practice of dance/movement as active imagination.

The author begins with her own story, through early dance studies and performing and teaching, to becoming a dance therapist and Jungian analyst. It is a story that shows, in an immediate way, how dance/movement is of value to psychotherapy: the emotions, their expression, and their role in psychological development are of utmost importance. A historical overview of Jung's basic concepts is given, as well as the most recent depth psychological synthesis of affect theory, based on the work of Silvan Tomkins, Louis Stewart, and others. Finally, in discussing the use of dance/movement as active imagination in the practice of psychotherapy, the movement themes that emerge and the nonverbal expressive aspects of the therapeutic relationship are described.

This delightful introduction to depth psychology from the perspective of body, psyche and the emotions will be of interest to practitioners, teachers and students of psychotherapy as well as those concerned with psychology and the arts.

Joan Chodorow Ph.D. is an analyst member of the C.G. Jung Institute of San Francisco, in private practice. Her early background includes dance studies and performing and teaching experience. Her dance therapy training was with Trudi Schoop and Mary Whitehouse. She is a registered dance therapist and former president of the American Dance Therapy Association.

DANCE THERAPY AND DEPTH PSYCHOLOGY

The moving imagination

JOAN CHODOROW

LONDON AND NEW YORK

First published 1991
by Routledge
11 New Fetter Lane, London EC4P 4EE

Reprinted 1991

Simultaneously published in the USA and Canada by
Routledge
a division of Routledge, Chapman and Hall, Inc.
29 West 35th Street, New York, NY 10001

Typeset by NWL Editorial Services, Langport, Somerset
Printed and bound in Great Britain by
Biddles Ltd, Guildford and King's Lynn

British Library Cataloguing in Publication Data
Chodorow, Joan
Dance therapy and depth psychology: the moving imagination
1. Psychoanalysis, Jungian systems
I. Title
150.1954

Library of Congress Cataloging in Publication Data
Chodorow, Joan, 1937–
Dance therapy and depth psychology: The moving imagination/
Joan Chodorow
p.   cm.
Includes bibliographical references
1. Dance therapy. 2. Psychoanalysis. 3. Jung, C.G. (Carl Gustav),
1875–1961. I. Title
RC489.D3C53   1990   90-8434
616.89'1655 — dc20   CIP

ISBN 0-415-05301-3
ISBN 0-415-04113-9 (pbk)

To Louis Herbert Stewart

CONTENTS

PLATES

ACKNOWLEDGEMENTS

This book began as a dissertation. I am grateful to the Scholarship Committee of the C.G. Jung Institute of San Francisco for a grant from the Ernst and Eleanor van Loben Sels Scholarship Fund. I received guidance and encouragement from an outstanding doctoral committee and extend my heartfelt thanks to each of them: John A. Buehler, Penny MacElveen-Hoehn, Carol McRae, Caroline Shrodes, Susan Snow and Phyllis Stowell. I would like also to express my deepest gratitude to Joseph L. Henderson, Louis H. Stewart and Nisha Zenoff, who served as consultants.

Consultations with Dr Henderson brought to life his concept of the cultural unconscious and its relationship to the external cultural forms. It was wonderful to learn how he developed his ideas and about his experiences with Jung. He read each chapter of the dissertation as I wrote it and responded with wisdom, critical intellect, humor, and encouragement. He is a splendid mentor. I can't thank him enough.

Grateful acknowledgement is made to Andrew Samuels for reading the dissertation and making valuable suggestions for expanding it into a book. His thoughts about changes to be made reflected, extended and clarified my own. In addition, other colleagues read the manuscript and responded with support, encouragement and constructive feedback. These individuals – Janet Adler, Connie Cook, Carolyn Grant Fay, Barbara McClintock, Renate Oppikofer, Tina Stromsted, Deborah Thomas, Wendy Wyman and James Yandell – all made important contributions to the development of this book.

Special thanks are due to Charles T. Stewart for making available to me his synthesis of the major developmental theories as well as studies that link development to the universal games children play. He brought to my attention a series of observations by

Piaget that demonstrate so clearly how the development of the imagination and the intellect go hand in hand. I want also to thank Peter Mudd who gave generously of his time and scholarship. His course materials that trace the evolution of Jung's concepts have been invaluable.

I wish to acknowledge the rich resource of historical and contemporary authors whose works have inspired me. My students have been another source of inspiration. I want to express special thanks to my patients and analysands. They have been my most important teachers and I'm deeply grateful. Descriptions of the movement themes of active imagination are drawn from many sources. Names and circumstantial details have been changed. I am grateful to those who contributed first-person narratives that express the experience of the mover, as well as those who gave me permission to write about them. Some of the themes I describe are drawn from a composite of many individuals. Much of this material appears here for the first time, but I have also drawn from previous publications. Quotations from dance therapy colleagues are acknowledged in the text. To all of the movers and all of the witnesses, thank you.

For the photographs I am indebted to Janet Adler, Carolyn Grant Fay, Jane Manning, Kathee Miller, Shira Musicant, Trudi Schoop, Ursula Weiss and Pauline Van Pelt for lending treasured photos from their collections. My special thanks to the photographers: Carolyn Caddes, Anne Harder, Hugo Lörtscher, Irving Manning, Chuck Newman, Ernest E. Reshovsky and Pauline Van Pelt.

Portions of the following papers and articles are interwoven throughout the book: 'The body as symbol: Dance/movement in analysis,' in *The Body in Analysis*, © 1986 Chiron Publications; 'To move and be moved,' in *Quadrant*, volume 17/2, 1984; 'An Interview with Joan Chodorow,' by Nancy Zenoff, in *The American Journal of Dance Therapy*, volume 9, 1986; and 'Dance therapy and the transcendent function,' in *The American Journal of Dance Therapy*, volume 2/1, 1978. I am grateful for permission to use the material.

In addition, I wish to acknowledge the warm support of kinship ties with family. To Eugene and Lillian Chodorow, Sarah, John and Benjamin Hawklyn, Rose Kleidman, Charles and Matilda Stewart, Daniel Stewart and Louis Stewart, my love and appreciation.

More than anyone, I want to thank Louis H. Stewart. It is a special pleasure to acknowledge his contribution because he is not only my respected colleague, he is also my husband. Although the responsibility for this work is clearly my own, it rests on his theoretical synthesis. His passion for the psyche, his dedication to scholarly inquiry, his love, support and playfulness – as well as his fine editorial eye and pencil made it all possible.

INTRODUCTION

Dance/movement and attention to the body experience in depth psychology are not new. Jung's early interest in the affects as bridge between body and psyche led him to observe carefully unconscious motor phenomena. His work with severely regressed patients led him to question and eventually discover the meaning of their symptomatic, expressive actions. In 1916 Jung wrote a paper that suggested expressive body movement is one of numerous ways to give form to the unconscious. In a description of the technique which he came to call active imagination he wrote that it could be done in any number of ways including dance, painting, drawing, work with clay and every other kind of artistic media. As with so many aspects of his work, he was far ahead of his time. The idea of using the arts as part of a psychotherapeutic process must have been startling in 1916. The original paper was circulated privately among some of Jung's students and remained unpublished until 1957 (Jung 1916, p. 67f). Still more time had to pass before the creative art therapies could emerge and be recognized by the mental health community.

The use of dance as a healing ritual goes back to earliest human history, but dance therapy is a relatively new profession. The American Dance Therapy Association, founded in 1966, defines dance therapy as the psychotherapeutic use of movement. Dance therapy is based on the assumption that mind and body are in constant reciprocal interaction (Schoop 1974, p. 44). It is built on psychological and physiological concepts that emphasize the relationship of body and psyche. 'Differences in theoretical conceptualizations may alter the style or technique, but the underlying movement theories are inclusive. Dance therapy offers an alternative method for working within the context of any systematized theory of human behavior' (Chaiklin 1975, p. 703).

1

This book will take an in-depth look at dance/movement as active imagination and provide a theoretical grounding for it in a classical and contemporary view of Jung's analytical psychology. The work is rooted in two traditions: depth psychology and dance therapy. Each offers rich resources to the other. Depth psychology gains a deeper understanding of the body experience and the language of expressive movement. Dance therapy gains a deeper understanding of the psyche in its personal, cultural and collective manifestations. Psychotherapy as a whole gains a valuable form of active imagination that has been largely neglected.

Part One, 'Personal Origins' is a narrative of my own development through dance to dance therapy. The natural unfolding of life has led me from an original enchantment with dance when I was 7 years of age to becoming a dancer, then teacher of dance, and finally a dance therapist, psychotherapist and Jungian analyst. In the course of these transitions I have become increasingly aware of the ways in which dance/movement as active imagination fosters the healing process in psychotherapy.

In Part Two, 'Depth Psychology and the Emotions,' I present a theory of the psyche that reflects, supports and differentiates my understanding of expressive movement. The troubled individual who comes to psychotherapy is suffering from emotional reactions that are disturbing and out of control. The therapist must therefore have an understanding of the nature of the emotions, their modes of expression, and their role in psychological development. In a sense, this section is a book within a book. I look at an historical and contemporary view of depth psychology with particular attention to the contributions of Jung, Henderson, Darwin, Tomkins and Stewart.

Part Three, 'The Moving Imagination,' shows the use of dance/movement as active imagination in the practice of psychotherapy. I describe the various levels of the psyche in conscious and unconscious aspects and try to differentiate the movement themes that emerge. I close with a discussion of psychotherapy and analysis, with particular attention to the nonverbal expressive aspects.

When working with the expressive movements of the body in psychotherapy, it is natural at times to become aware of sexual energy and concerns about sexualizing the therapeutic relationship. Actually, these concerns are no different from those experienced in any type of psychotherapy or analysis. Any depth psychological process leads to experiences of the instincts and affects. Naturally, the psychotherapist needs to understand the power of the transference and hold clear boundaries. A psychotherapeutic relationship, by definition, cannot be a sexual relationship. To permit that is destructive, a betrayal of trust. This dimension of the therapeutic relationship has recently been dealt with in a deeply sensitive way by Peter Rutter in his book, *Sex in the forbidden zone*(1989).

In what follows I fluctuate between descriptive material that is easy to read and theoretical material that is much more complicated. It occurs to me that it might be helpful to the reader if I outline in advance certain major themes that appear and reappear throughout.

In the course of my work with movement, I've been drawn inevitably to grapple with questions about the mysterious interface that mediates between body and psyche. Jung calls this the psychoid level. He describes it as a transformative function in the depths of the unconscious that mediates between the realms of body and psyche, instinct and image. It seems obvious that the emotions are the stuff of that interface. An emotion, by definition, is at once somatic and psychic. The somatic aspect is made up of bodily innervations and expressive physical action. The psychic aspect is made up of images and ideas. In psychopathology, the two realms tend to split. By contrast, a naturally felt emotion involves a dialectical relationship – a union of body and psyche.

The fundamental emotions: Joy, Excitement, Grief, Fear, Anger, Contempt, Shame, Surprise are innate patterns of expressive behavior. They interweave throughout every part of the book. In part one I describe them in the context of intense, imaginative movement experience. Dance and choreography are engaged with all of the fundamental emotions. The expressive patterns are at once personal and universal. Whether the emotions are named or not, they motivate and shape the way we move. I describe how dance therapy studies too are completely involved with the expression and transformation of the emotions. Sometimes, intense affects erupt spontaneously out of a deeply introverted, self-directed movement process. Other times, the emotions are symbolically enacted. Dance therapy studies and practice led me to see that every emotion has survival value as well as a spiritual dimension. But the same emotions, when repressed and denied, can restrict and distort the body. In the narrative I try also to describe the impacted expressions of the fundamental emotions that seemed to be frozen into the faces and bodies of many of the chronic schizophrenic patients I worked with.

An important part of understanding the nature of the emotions is that each has its own range of intensity. For example, the lower intensities of Fear are uncertainty, uneasiness, apprehension and anxiety. The higher intensities of Fear are panic and terror. As you read this material, if you can stand it, let yourself remember and imagine the bodily innervations (heart pounding, dry mouth, cold perspiration, loose bowels, hairs-on-end) and the typical expressive actions (jumpiness, running, trembling, wide-open-eyes, gasping, recoil, cowering, motionless) that are part of the universal pattern of Fear. If you just imagined your way through that, you may still be feeling it in your body. To get back to normal you might try taking a deep breath (and let it go). Also, let yourself stretch and yawn. To read and think and imagine around the crisis emotions takes a lot of energy. Some of us feel things deeply when we read. Others may ward off intense feelings by taking on an attitude of clinical detachment. But whether your tendency is toward merging or detachment, I ask you to be aware that we're working with highly charged material. In a sense, the innate affects are the most primitive gods. Even as we name them, they demand our attention, care and respect.

In the theoretical section, I show how Jung's psychological theory was built on his early studies of the emotionally toned complex. Whereas Freud emphasized the drives as the source of human motivation, Jung held to the primacy of the emotions. I take up the structure of the psyche including Henderson's concept of the cultural unconscious in some detail, to lay the groundwork for my later discussion of movement themes. Obviously, movement at any moment is not necessarily from a single level of the psyche. Every expressive action reflects the individual mover's attempt to cope dynamically with myriad impulses and images that come from many sources. The process of active imagination in movement is extremely complex. But with careful attention, one begins to see patterns. Movement from the personal unconscious can serve as an embodied link to an individual's past. Movement from the cultural unconscious is our bridge to mythic images and the development of cultural forms. Movement from the primordial unconscious may, for brief moments, put us in touch with the completely untransformed primal affects. Movement from the ego-Self axis of identity gives us the experience of being moved by the ordering and centering process of the psyche.

Following the introduction to some of Jung's basic ideas, I take up Darwin's early study of the fundamental emotions (1872) and the major contribution by Tomkins (1962, 1963) nearly a century later. Darwin's study is a wonder of detailed description of every pattern of expressive behavior in animals and humans. His ability to observe, describe and analyze movement behavior led him to differentiate between the fundamental emotions (which are innate) and the complex emotions. Darwin points out that complex emotions lack a prototypical pattern of expressive behavior. That means they cannot be 'read' by facial or bodily expression alone. For example, a person may be filled with the most intense jealousy, but it does not lead immediately to physical action. Jealousy ordinarily lasts for a long time. Its outward expression tends to be idiosyncratic. When jealous passion erupts into physical action, it usually becomes Rage, perhaps with fluctuations of Contempt, Shame and Grief. But the nonverbal expressive behavior of jealousy tends to be indistinct. On the body level, all of the complex emotions are difficult to recognize or describe, so we are largely guided by our general or intuitive knowledge of the situation.

Although Darwin knew that emotions are felt and expressed over a wide range of intensity, he didn't organize or formulate them that way in his book. Tomkins was the first to recognize that there are a limited number of innate affects and he presents each as a continuum of intensity. I gave the example above of Apprehension–Fear–Terror. In dance therapy studies I remember progressions across the studio floor that explored each fundamental affect in its range of intensity. For example, we would begin with a life situation that evokes irritation, then builds to frustration, anger and finally explodes in Rage. We would also do it the other way around. Dance therapists have been working for years with the same emotions Tomkins identifies, but we came to them through our own movement experience and work with patients.

After the review of studies of the individual emotions, I present Stewart's synthesis of Jung and Tomkins. Building on the innate emotions as the foundation of the psyche, Stewart proposes a new hypothesis that takes up specific affects and the specific higher functions that appear to have evolved from them. He is the first to identify the affective source of the primordial Self (Fear, Grief, Anger, Contempt/Shame), the affective source of the libido that modulates and transforms it (Joy, Interest), the affective source of the centering process (Startle), and the affective nature of the higher Self (Ego Functions and Cultural Attitudes). This material offers an embodied, integrated sense of the Self in its unconscious

5

and conscious aspects as it develops from the primal, untransformed depths toward the ultimate goal of self-realization.

Interwoven throughout the book are my experiences, informed by Stewart's research about the natural, healing function of the imagination and the ongoing, dialectical relationship between curiosity and imagination. The spontaneous, symbolic play of childhood offers the model. Children play for the fun of it, but as we know, the content of symbolic play usually recapitulates challenging, difficult or upsetting life experiences. In play, children will change the actual situation by reversing roles, trying out different solutions and coming up with infinite variations and creative resolutions of the theme. These dramatic enactments are completely voluntary. No matter how upsetting the content, children would normally rather play than do anything else.

The condition of play is that we are free to be completely ourselves. To play and imagine is to be open to anything and everything that occurs to us. That's why symbolic play and imagination may put us on a collision course with thoughts, feelings and fantasies that have been repressed.

In psychotherapy, the first thing to keep in mind about the imagination is that it tends to take us directly to the emotional core of our complexes. This happens whether we sit in chairs and speak freely without censoring, or draw pictures, sculpt, do sandplay or move. It also happens when we have fantasies around the therapeutic relationship, or engage in silent dialogues with inner figures. When we use our bodies to express the imagination, the vividness of the sensory-motor experience tends to take us to complexes that were constellated in infancy or early childhood.

The second thing to remember about the nature of the imagination is that it's a symbolic process. Just as the imagination takes us *to* the emotional core of a complex, it can also lead us *through* it. But at this point, we have to be alert, attentive and interested in what we are imagining. This means developing the ability to bear the emotion that is stirred when a complex is touched, and at the same time imagine and explore symbolically the images that are part of it.

Every form of active imagination initiates this essential dialogue between curiosity and imagination. Such a dialogue is an interweaving of conscious and unconscious; it is the ultimate source of creativity. The creative process that is intrinsic to children and their development is the same process that fosters individuation in an adult in psychotherapy. Of course Jung discovered the intimate relationship between the play of imagination and the individuation process many years ago. He found in his own experience, and that of his patients, that turning to play and the imagination with an active attitude of receptivity to unconscious fantasies sets in motion a process which can only be understood as a counterpart of the innate creative process; it guides development in the child, is the source of our most valued cultural achievements, and in psychotherapy re-creates the wholeness of personality with which we entered this world.

The theme of mirroring will be found in every part of this book. Infants and young children mirror everything they see through the movement of their bodies. Mirroring, as emotional attunement, draws attention to an essential ingredient of the psychotherapeutic process. I am speaking of the dialectical relationship which of necessity exists between patient and therapist. The troubled individual, child or adult, who comes to see a psychotherapist has suffered a blockage or damage of the creative dialogue we have discussed above. The suffering individual needs the presence of an empathic person who can provide a *temenos*, a safe and secure space, within which unconscious fantasies and conscious dilemmas can be safely dealt with. The nature of this dialectic between patient and therapist is fostered by an empathic mirroring on the part of the therapist. This subject, in its broadest sense, is known as transference and countertransference. It is a huge one which needs much further study. It is my belief, however, that through observations of dance/movement we have an opportunity to learn much about the subtleties of the dialectic of expressive movement that goes on between patient and psychotherapist. In the end it is our ability as psychotherapists to recognize and mirror empathically the expressive reactions of our patients which is fundamental to the success of psychotherapy. As Jung has observed in this regard:

The unrelated human being lacks wholeness, for he can achieve wholeness only through the soul, and the soul cannot exist without its other side, which is always found in a 'You.' Wholeness is a combination of I and You, and these show themselves to be parts of a transcendent unity whose nature can only be grasped symbolically ...

(1946, pp. 244–5).

Part One

PERSONAL ORIGINS

Chapter One

DANCE TO DANCE THERAPY

I took my first ballet lesson when I was 7, with Jane Denham, a wonderful young teacher who knew how to interweave a foundation of classical technique with time each class for free dance improvisation. Each child in turn entered a 'magic circle' where she could enter a pretend world and interact with or become any kind of imaginal being. For me, dance became not only an engrossing and challenging discipline, but also the purest form of imaginative play.

As I entered my teen years, I began intensive studies with Carmelita Maracci, a great artist and teacher. Her daily classes became the center of my life. She demanded utter dedication from her students and imparted an unusually strong classical ballet technique. But technique was never an end in itself, rather it was necessary to give form to powerful images, to express the heights and depths of human experience. Music, emotion and dance were inseparable. Carmelita's accompanists were usually pianists of concert caliber who played with great feeling. The beauty of the music moved many of her students to tears, so it was not unusual to dance and at the same time weep. Transcending the pain of aching muscles and blistered, sometimes bleeding toes that is part of a young dancer's life, added even higher intensity to the expressive quality.

Then I became a professional dancer and experienced a very different approach to dance. For a number of years I took the jobs that were available. That meant dancing in nightclubs, musical comedy and other forms of popular entertainment. Some of the work was wonderful, particularly when I had the privilege of working with a fine choreographer. But most of it was depressing – far from the imaginative, emotional experiences that had made me want to dance in the first place.

11

I began to teach. At first it was just between performing jobs. But in time, teaching felt more alive to me than performing. Teaching dance, particularly to children, helped me re-connect to an essential creative source.

The shift into full-time teaching occurred in my early twenties. I opened my own school in East Los Angeles and also taught classes in other schools and centers throughout the city. I loved teaching and tried to offer the children I worked with the same rich foundation of classical technique and imaginative play that had been important to me. At first, my orientation was to make professional dancers. Then, my world turned around completely when I was asked to teach a group of 3-year-olds. They were too young to learn any kind of ballet technique, so I had to find a new way of working. As I watched them, I realized that everything they did was a mirroring of the world in movement: while they were watching something, they would imitate it. When they remembered something, they enacted the memory. It was a revelation for me to realize that children learned about the world and about themselves through their bodies.

They liked bugs. So we paid careful attention to the bugs we found and developed a series of 'bug walks' that we did across the length of the studio. Whenever one of the children had a cut or scratch, all of the other children were intensely interested in it. We began to spend part of each class going round the circle while everyone took a turn to show their most recent 'hurt' and demonstrate how it had happened, in mime. We built cities, using imaginary tools and materials. We danced our way through every kind of holiday celebration, pretending to prepare the food, pretending to get dressed-up in the national costumes, and enacting the stories of that culture. We pretended to be every kind of wild animal. We also danced our pets. We pretended to be teachers, mothers, fathers, older and younger siblings. We danced being caterpillars and wove ourselves into cocoons where we slept peacefully until it was time to struggle our way out of the cocoon and emerge (to our own great astonishment) as butterflies. 'Dance' and 'pretend' were synonymous.

From working with such young children in the dance studio, I became increasingly interested in dance for children in nursery school programs. My studio was across the street from Height's Cooperative Nursery School. I began a collaboration with Ethel Young who was the Director. We developed some of the early courses and written materials for teachers on the role of the arts in early childhood education. All of the arts – dance, painting, clay, dress-up – were seen as many languages through which the children could express and interpret their experiences. Ethel helped me understand that the process we call child development is completely interwoven with the creative process. Those years of work with very young children, and their parents and teachers, gave me an understanding of development that has been essential to every aspect of my work as a dance therapist, psychotherapist and Jungian analyst.

Sometime in the early 1960s, a social worker from Los Angeles County General Hospital came to the nursery school looking for an enrichment program for one of the autistic children on the psychiatric unit. She watched me move with the children in one of the dance groups and invited me to come to the psychiatric unit and work with the children there. At that time, I had no psychological training.

The first day I went up to the sixth floor of a very old building. The doors were locked. About fifteen children between the ages of 3 and 12 were in treatment there. Most of them were psychotic. Some were also blind, some were deaf. Some actively withdrew from contact. Others wanted to be held and hugged, but not for very long. One child tugged to get the attention of any adult he could find. He then pulled them to where there was something he wanted, but couldn't get by himself. After pointing to it and making urgent sounds, he usually got it. He then did his best to try to stuff the new treasure in his mouth or inside his shirt or pants. Another child, perhaps 8 years old, walked around saying in a monotone: 'I'm very angry. I'm a very angry boy.'

The day room had peeling yellow paint on the walls and old fashioned radiators. I walked in with a portable phonograph, records, scarves and a drum. One of the tired women attendants looked on. Some of the children were sitting, staring and talking to themselves. One little girl walked on her toes with her eyes rolled back. I couldn't tell whether or not she was blind. There was a lot of activity along the window wall where a whole group of children were climbing on and off the radiators.

Somehow, I had the sense that if I could just put on wonderful music, it would change everything. As I remember, I put on a Russian Hopak. Some of the staff and some of the children liked the music. We got into a loose circle, with the children moving in and out of it. Some of the kids were shrieking and boisterous. As I said, the circle was very loose – we just started running around, more or less in the same direction. We were stamping and doing different kinds of clapping and other things, and more children joined in. Now one of the boys who had been climbing the radiators joined us, but he didn't want to do what we were doing – he wanted to bark. Another boy joined him and soon they were both scrambling around on all fours, barking. Since that was becoming the most interesting thing going on, I too got down on my hands and knees and the rest of the children followed. I hoped we would soon all be barking and scrambling in some kind of synchrony, but then a little girl wandered off, one of the children on her toes with her eyes rolled back. Hoping to invite her back into the group, I took off the Hopak, put on a Debussy piece that sounds like clouds, and passed out the scarves. Since many of the children liked to stuff things inside themselves, a lot of the scarves disappeared under clothes, into mouths and ears and other body openings. Yet somehow, the energy and music and movement kept us connected. Later when I put on a Mexican Hat Dance, the children liked it and some of the attendants who had been watching smiled, and joined the dancing. At this point, 'dancing' meant jumping, stamping and running around a circle that had an imaginary hat in the center of it. But the music held it together and the session ended with children, attendants and some of the therapists dancing in partners and *en masse*. When it was over, some of the children clapped and cheered, others climbed back on the radiators and stared into space, others wandered off and mumbled to themselves. The tired looking attendants clapped and smiled. The chief psychiatrist had been watching through the one-way glass. Someone reported his comments to me: 'The children have never gotten such good exercise. She's a gem. Hire her.'

The following years were a major transition time. What contained it all was an analysis with Dr Kate Marcus, one of the founders of the C.G. Jung Institute of Los Angeles. I had always been curious about psychoanalysis and felt especially drawn to Jung's psychology. But it was not my fascination with the unconscious that brought me into analysis, it was a life crisis. At the age of 24, I found myself in the midst of a bitter divorce. I had to find the resources to support my young daughter and myself. Two or three times a week, I sat in a chair across from a wise old woman. We talked about dreams. The integrity of that work remains with me. It served as a base and model for much subsequent growth.

I continued to teach in my storefront ballet studio in East Los Angeles as well as in a number of nursery schools and private elementary schools. But my direction had clarified. I was no longer interested in training professional dancers. Instead, I wanted to learn all I could about the therapeutic aspects of dance and the creative process. I continued to work with Ethel Young on the arts and child development. In addition to teaching, I began to do an increasing amount of therapeutic work at the hospital; developed some dance and movement programs for learning-disabled children at a number of special schools; and did some individual work with emotionally disturbed children, adolescents and adults. During this period, I began and continued intensive studies with Trudi Schoop and Mary Whitehouse, two of the major pioneers of dance therapy.

Chapter Two

TRUDI SCHOOP

I had taken my first class from Trudi Schoop when I was 19. She was a world famous dancer and pantomime artist who was beginning to bring her profound understanding of human expression and her marvelous sense of humor into the wards of psychiatric hospitals.

That first meeting had been in 1956 when she was teaching a class in 'Improvisation' at Dance Center on Western Avenue in Los Angeles. I had been teaching ballet classes there. I signed up to take her class, along with most of the other members of the Dance Center faculty, as well as students.

After an energetic warm-up, she led us through a series of progressions in a long diagonal across the studio floor, one after the other. We improvised around a variety of sensory images, i.e. played with imaginary balls of different sizes and weights, did lop-sided walks as we struggled to carry an imaginary suitcase. We then began to imagine more freely and went on to explore and express the widest range of dramatic and emotional experiences.

As I think back to that afternoon, I realize I was thrilled, yet at the same time increasingly uneasy. As a ballet dancer I was used to being in control of my body. I loved to improvise, but was more comfortable with themes that could be expressed through the stylized vocabulary of ballet.

Trudi's class demanded more than I could handle at the time. At a certain point, I lost touch with the motivating images. It seemed to me that people were simply giving themselves over to the compelling, rhythmic music and letting it carry them across the room. When it was my turn, I felt a moment of panic – and then hurled myself into space. I must have become unconscious, because I couldn't remember what I had done. I just found myself landing on both feet, hard, on the other side of the room. I was out of breath. My heart was pounding. I was shocked, almost numb. I had a terrible feeling that somehow my ultimate shadow had emerged and I hadn't seen it, but everyone else had. I felt embarrassed and awkward, but didn't want anyone to know how bad I felt. So I just kept going in the same direction, around the piano, up the steps and into the dressing room. I pulled some street clothes on over my leotards and left. It took five years of growing up before I felt ready to come back and study with Trudi Schoop.

In the early 1960s, she began to train a small group of students who wanted to learn about dance therapy. By then, I felt ready and eager to immerse myself in studies with her. We met regularly at a large, professional dance studio in Van Nuys where Trudi taught her classes. We also participated in group dance therapy sessions she led at Camarillo State Hospital.

The first time I went there, I was struck to realize that many of the patients assumed that Trudi too, was a patient. Most staff people wore uniforms then, or at least white jackets. The professional staff tended to wear formal looking street clothes. But Trudi was dressed to move. She (and her students) wore an odd but colorful assortment of dancewear and loose fitting garments. Another reason she was seen and accepted as if she were a fellow patient is her completely unpretentious attitude. There is no professional persona. She is simply herself.

When we went to the hospital, Trudi led two or three sessions, one after the other, each with a different small group. Most of the patients she worked with were diagnosed chronic schizophrenics. Many were mute and engaged in various, perseverative actions: some of the actions were relatively safe, others were self-destructive or threatening to others. As we entered one of the back wards of women, there was a loud banging sound, like the slow reverberation of a drum beat. A heavy set, middle-aged woman with hard, staring eyes sat on the floor with her back to the wall. With great force, she was repeatedly crashing her back against the wall. Another woman there had skin that was raw from constant hand wringing. In the men's ward, a man walked around in a seemingly frozen state of fear: tense, raised shoulders, bulging eyes, open mouth. Another man walked in a shuffle, with his legs turning inward toward each other. One hand covered his face, while the other arm stayed close to his body in a shrinking, constricted gesture that felt like shame. I remember also a catatonic woman with eyebrows raised and open mouth, as if suspended in a perpetual state of astonishment. So many of the patients seemed to be living their whole life through the filter of a single primal emotion. Trudi had first noticed this in her native Switzerland:

> How vividly I remember Professor Bleuler's patients in Zurich when, many years ago, he asked me to perform for them. How black and white were their expressions – without any shading – only angry, only fearful, only ....
> (Schoop 1974, p. 16)

As she developed her work, she became aware of other patients whose bodies were split.

> I remembered Bleuler talking about *die Spaltung* – 'The Split.' I was now seeing in the schizophrenic body the term he used to define the schizophrenic mind. They were split in tension; they were split in expression. Soft, smiling face was mounted on stiff, stubborn body. Angry, contracted feet belied tender, limp hands. A boldly thrust out chest loomed over a weak, collapsed pelvis. These separations seem to occur in every element of movement, or in any combination of elements.
> (Schoop 1974, p. 107)

Now in the United States, she was no longer performing, but making a major contribution to the development of a new profession, dance therapy. As a dancer, she had studied the body, just as others study the mind. Her keen observation skills led her to see in detail the enormous distortions, contractions and cramps in the bodies of her patients. She realized that if she could change the body, there would be a corresponding change in the mind.

> The body can influence even the desperately disturbed mind of the psychotic patient. The attempt to transform his unfunctional physical distortions presents an enormous challenge, but I must try, and I want to try, to reestablish for him a body that will again operate effectively, perform normally, one that will have a positive, remedial effect upon his mind.
> (Schoop 1974, p. 45)

Trudi usually began her groups with some kind of rhythmic movement, with attention to different body parts. Such a warm-up might look like simple directed exercises: head going up-down, side to side; shoulders lifting and dropping, then elbows, then hands. Then, everyone stood in a circle and held hands to balance themselves as they did leg swings. Arm swings would lead to whole body swings: whole body swings would lead into jumps. She did everything possible to get people to be *conscious* of their bodies and help them *extend their range* of movement possibilities. Some of the groups were able to go from such structured forms into a more spontaneous 'follow the leader' game, where each person took a turn to do whatever they liked to do.

It is always astonishing to see the utter transformation that occurs in dance therapy groups. The most regressed people come to life, as they begin to move and play and laugh together. Trudi led her groups through various situations in pantomime. For example, standing in a large circle, she went around from one to the other, showing each person that she liked them very much. Then she asked each person to: 'Do it in your own way.' Here, people turned to a wide variety of cultural forms for friendly greetings. One made a slight bow to each person, as he went round the circle. Another shook hands. One man hugged everyone. Another put his hand on the other's shoulder. She also demonstrated how people reject each other. Again, everyone in the group turned to such culturally understandable forms as turning their heads away, or wrinkling (or holding) their noses, or shaking their head slowly side to side as if saying a quiet but clear 'No.' One man walked up to each person in the circle, then suddenly turned his back on them. Another man went around the circle, pushing everyone away.

Some of the groups that had been working together for a while, developed a wonderful capacity spontaneously to enter into and play with any image. Patients enacted and even choreographed their visions. Sometimes the content was filled with terror and ugliness. Other times the fantasy worlds were friendly and golden. Alice was a patient who withdrew from her life in the hospital by going far away to be with her friends on Venus. Trudi wrote about the day when Alice invited the group to enact her fantasy:

'How would it be, Alice,' I asked one day, 'if you would tell all of us here in the group how your friends look and what they do that makes you love them so much?'

'Well ...,' she began hesitantly, 'they're all so happy to see me when I come up to them. And sometimes Clandestine gives me a kiss.'

Nobody in the group had to be told what to do. Awkwardly

but with affection, they shook Alice's hand. They patted her. They smiled. Their greetings must have pleased her, because she continued her description .... Alice began to teach her willing cast how these beautiful people moved and flew and drank and played ....

Alice knew, in the session that day, that she was in the hospital studio, not on Venus, and that the one who kissed her was good old Betty, not Clandestine. But weren't these earth people responding to her in much the same way as her planetary friends? Perhaps it would not be so necessary to take refuge on that other planet. Perhaps reality was not so bad after all!

(Schoop 1974, pp. 148–9)

The groups ended in many ways. Sometimes they ended with a climax of activity with movements of running, skipping, prancing, stamping, kicking. Other times, they ended in a more quiet, reflective mood. There was a time when Trudi put on an especially beautiful piece of music, a polonaise. We pretended to dress up like ladies of the eighteenth century, with long gowns and sparkling jewels. The gentlemen too, were dressed in fine garments. They wore elegant boots and powdered wigs. All of us carried our heads with special care, so as not to lose our imaginary headdresses or wigs. We seemed to have all the time in the world to greet each other and linger on, as we danced around one another in a stately promenade.

She worked individually with those who were so out of contact that they couldn't function in a group. There was a mute woman who could only pace, so the sessions consisted of pacing together in a room almost every day. After eight months, the pacing had gradually become a kind of rhythmic, playful interaction. Finally, the woman was able to speak (Schoop 1974, pp. 73–5).

Back in the studio, Trudi and her students talked about what we had seen at the hospital. As we talked, we 'tried on' the gait and posture, of every patient we could remember, trying to imagine and feel what the corresponding state of mind might be. Most of the postural configurations were extremely uncomfortable. It felt almost unbearable to imagine how a person might experience life from such a cramped, distorted body. To imagine waking up and going through every part of my day literally 'sticking my chin out,' with elbows held back and fists tight – has a profound effect on the way I perceive the world. If I were living inside such a body, everything would be felt as a threat.

20

To study with Trudi is to get fascinated by every aspect of human expression. Her students began to 'try on' every kind of movement, including the way friends and family members moved. As classmates, we observed and 'tried on' each other's gait and posture. We exaggerated what we saw and described what it felt like. My classmates let me know that although my walk was smooth and graceful, they felt constrained when they tried to do it. I came to realize that as I walked, my body tended to lean slightly backward. The constrained feelings had to do with a particular kind of body split. I realized that even though I moved forward, I maintained a subtle attitude of avoidance and retreat. That is a complicated tension to live with. Yet I had been doing it for years, without consciousness. When Trudi asked me to exaggerate the movements and show more of what I was feeling, I realized I wanted to keep some distance between myself and others. As I walked, I gave this feeling form by slowly raising my arms and pushing away with my hands. For the next several months, it was astonishing to become aware of the memories and emotions that had been carried by this posture. A subtle sense of aloneness was woven throughout every aspect of my life. When I tried to make a deliberate change, i.e. by making myself stand in a more vertical axis, it felt as if everything and everyone was suddenly too close for comfort. I decided to settle back into my more familiar distancing stance. But consciousness changes everything. As I became increasingly aware of my tendency to lean backwards, I began to experience it emotionally as fluctuations between shyness and contempt. As the somatic state took on psychological meaning, I could feel the emotions directly. My body didn't have to carry them. Gradually, in a way that felt natural, my walk changed.

Trudi was interested in fostering congruency between intention and action. When we ran, she wanted *everything* in the body to support the running. If we were turning, she wanted every part of the body to be involved with turning. Nothing should drag back. On the other hand, if we felt indecisive, every part of the body should participate in expressing the split. She put a very high value on *clarity of expression*.

We got to know the parts of our bodies we liked best – and the parts we disliked. We played with showing off what we liked and hiding what we disliked.

We tried to imagine and remember how our parents were in their bodies. How did they move? What did they like and dislike about themselves?

We improvised around the qualities in our own movements that had pleased our parents, and what upset them. We tried to imagine how we would move if it were simply to please ourselves.

In our studies, we explored the prototypical expressive actions of every primal affect. Trudi would ask: 'How do you move when you're afraid?' We took turns going across the room, imagining (or remembering) a fearful life experience and our response to it. At first, we must have looked fairly inhibited in our expression, so Trudi developed the image further. Instead of being afraid as *one's self*, she asked us to imagine: 'It is many thousands of years ago. You are the first humans on earth. Can you imagine what you would feel and do if, for the first time, without warning, you hear the sound of thunder?' Now the universal, primal expression could erupt through us. When I imagined the crack of thunder, I fell to the ground. In that moment, I first understood the link between fear and the voice of God.

To express anger, she began by asking us to move as we do when we're angry. Most of us remembered and expressed irritation, or exasperation – or we showed the way we struggle to control anger. Then, Trudi asked us to do it again: 'Now, you have the *right* to be angry!' That changed everything. With a great release of energy, most of us began to punch, poke, kick and slash. Her next direction was: 'Take all of that energy and transform it into a beautiful dance.' Suddenly the studio was filled with stamping, leaping Cossacks, Spanish dancers doing intricate heel work, a variety of African and Indian war dances, and stylizations of exploding fireworks and erupting volcanoes.

Such intensive studies went on over a period of several years. We discovered each of our five senses – as if for the first time. We grew ourselves through the stages of infancy to all of the life stages that follow. We danced the history of life on planet earth, from the growing and shrinking movements of amoeba in primordial swamps – to the swinging, climbing movements of our monkey ancestors, to the wonder and terror of being the first humans on earth, to the gradual accumulation of inhibitions we see in ourselves and others all around us nowadays, both in and out of the hospital.

Trudi questioned, challenged and supported her students in every way. She urged us to consider carefully the reasons why we wanted to become therapists. She never used the phrase 'wounded healer.' But in a thousand ways, she emphasized that a therapist must know why she does therapy – that the decision to do this kind

of work must come out of self knowledge. Years later, at a ceremony in her honor, Trudi spoke about this issue on a more personal level (Schoop 1983). She spoke about her childhood
experience of being consumed by unknown terrors. As a girl, her
life was gradually taken over by strange compulsive actions, rituals
to appease threatening gods. She lost weight. Sanatoriums had
little to offer. Then she began to study drama which led to her
realization that she wanted to dance. She locked herself in a room
after school and composed dances. Dance was her own transformative healing process.

This brief narrative cannot do justice to the richness of her
work. By mirroring, she taught us about the deepest levels of empathic response. She brought consciousness to the emotional con-
flicts that had been stored in the musculature. To initiate change,
she showed that it is the *fulfillment* of the action that makes the link
to inner experience. And woven throughout everything was the
relationship of the body, the imagination and the emotions.

I shall close with Trudi's summary statement of her goals:

1 To identify for each person the specific parts of his body that
  have been unused or misused, and to direct his actions into
  functional patterns.
2 To establish the unifying interactive relationship between
  mind and body, between fantasy and reality.
3 To bring subjective emotional conflict into an objective
  physical form, where it can be perceived and dealt with
  constructively.
4 To use every aspect of movement that will increase the
  individual's ability to adapt adequately to his environment
  and to experience himself as a whole, functioning human
  being.

  These are my facts. They compose the theory I couldn't
explain ... many long years ago. But somehow, there is one
very important something missing – the very spirit of dance
itself. But there are just no words to impart the measureless
sense of joy, the love of life, the enchantment with existence
that envelops the dancing human.

Have you danced lately?

(Schoop 1974, pp. 157–8)

Chapter Three

MARY STARKS WHITEHOUSE

It was an entirely different experience to study with Mary. She did not work in a hospital or clinic. She did not work with people who were psychotic. She worked with well functioning 'normal neurotics' in a studio on Santa Monica Boulevard in West Los Angeles. She shared the studio with Jane Manning, a younger colleague who had studied with her. The studio environment provided an unusually quiet, clean, clear space. There was little socializing. As each person entered, they would find a space in the room, lie on the floor, close their eyes, and wait – or begin to warm-up on their own. Mary Whitehouse was developing an approach that was based on Jung's active imagination. Sometimes called 'Authentic Movement' or 'Movement-in-Depth,' it involved a process of deep inner listening toward expressive movement that was spontaneous – unplanned. People generally moved with their eyes closed, or with an inward focus. At first, people were invited simply to immerse in the experience, without need for reflection. But in time her students learned to yield to the ongoing stream of bodily felt sensations and images, while at the same time bringing the experience into conscious awareness. She offered ongoing groups as well as work with individuals. She also gave weekend workshops and training groups for teachers and therapists who wanted to learn about her approach.

Mary Whitehouse had studied with Mary Wigman and Martha Graham. She had danced in concert and was a teacher of modern dance. She entered a Jungian analysis with Hilda Kirsch in Los Angeles, then studied at the Jung Institute in Zurich. She was the first to link a thorough understanding of dance and movement to the principles of depth psychology. In her paper, 'Reflections on a Metamorphosis,' she described the change in herself:

It was an important day when I discovered that I did not teach Dance; I taught People .... It indicated a possibility that my primary interest might have to do with process not results, that it might not be art I was after but another kind of human development.

(Whitehouse 1968, p. 273)

When I began to study with her in 1962, I still tended toward deliberate, stylized movement. In the early months of our work, I'd start to move and she would say, 'No!' Then I'd wait, and start to move again, and she would say, 'No!' This happened so many times that I did much more waiting than moving. Then, I gradually realized that I could truly *let* something happen. I didn't have to form the movement consciously. It had its own form. I learned that I could listen to my body, and something would happen, then something else would happen.

It was similar to the way I was working with dreams in my analysis, where you would take an image and give it your attention, and as you give it your attention, it changes. And then you give it more attention and see what develops out of that. Mary taught me to pay attention to and move from images and bodily felt sensations. You would wait to see what comes up and follow it, and then you would find yourself in a different inner landscape, interacting with whoever or whatever appears.

She began her classes with modern dance floor work, i.e., sitting on the floor and going through a series of warm-up exercises. But her warm-ups gave more attention to detail than I had ever experienced. She wanted her students to sense the quality of the movement, with particular attention to the transitions. For example, if we were doing a combination that involved arms lifting above our heads, separating and opening, she might break it down to the tiny piece of movement that occurs in that split second when the arms reach utmost height and begin to separate. We would linger with that moment and work with it over and over. In her wish to bring consciousness to the body, she asked her students to listen to what the movement feels like from inside.

Mary often suggested specific themes to explore in movement. For example, could we use movement to find the relationship between a pair of opposites such as: open and closed (or, up and down, tight and loose, left and right, push and pull, etc.)? Whether I began by standing, sitting, or lying on the ground, it was always an amazing experience to open my body as far as it wanted to

25

open, and then feel the moment when the opening completed it-self and with an inevitable quality, turn into its opposite. Then, as I continued to close, the moment would come when the closing was complete and there would be another turnaround. To do such sustained, in-depth work with any pair of opposites leads the mover to a powerful, fully embodied experience of polarity and a dynamic interrelationship of the opposites. Mary rarely spoke of the *Tao* in class, but she knew that the body, as well as the psyche is formed through the tension of many pairs of opposites. Any conscious human action requires the operation of at least two muscles, one contracting, one extending. Each body axis is organized by a pair of opposites: a three-dimensional being exists simultaneously in the vertical (up-down), lateral (left-right), and sagittal (forward-backward) axes. If we consciously attend to the simplest body movement, we will experience the interrelationship and interdependency of the opposites.

Other themes she suggested were similar to the nature images nursery school children had taught me to pay attention to. For example, she asked us to improvise around the theme of a seed growing:

I became the seed, lying in darkness, surrounded by moist earth. My body shape was condensed, knees-to-chest, arms wrapping around myself. I knelt, facing the ground, my back faced toward the sky. As I waited, the center of my back became a kind of focal point. It was as if the center of my back was drawn up toward the light – slightly rocking and swaying to reach upward. Part of me wanted to keep rising and eventually stand. But it became difficult to do, as if the 'eye' in the middle of my back wanted to keep 'looking' at the sky. I waited with this tension a long time. Then, without thought or plan, my head dove down and one of my legs stretched straight up. Suspended on one knee, I was in a kind of upside-down arabesque. The center of my back was at a diagonal to the sky. The rebound brought me easily to my feet, like a burst of affirmation. Constant surprise, this work.

(Chodorow, n.d.)

She also suggested themes that were specific to the needs of an individual. Here she describes a powerful transition in a one-to-one session.

26

A woman stood alone in the center of the studio. It was her third or fourth appointment. We had been working very simply with stretching, bending, standing and walking. Her movement in general existed in a cloud over her head – the face and eyes nearly always turned up to the ceiling, the arms and hands repeatedly extended overhead, the weight lifted up on the toes, everything going up, nothing down, everything going out, nothing held. I suggested she clench her fists and bring them up from her sides in front of her. The first time, the hands closed but there was very little tension in the muscles of the arms, they still floated. The second time she waited longer and pulled harder. Very slowly the arms bent at the elbows, closing upward in front of her body. As the fists approached her face, her expression became one of intense sorrow and strain, and at the point of almost touching her own mouth and cheeks, the whole body turned and pitched downward onto the floor in a violent fall, and she burst into long sobs. A barrier had been pierced, a dam broken, her body had pitched her into feeling.

(Whitehouse 1958)

Perhaps Mary's greatest contribution to understanding body movement as a form of active imagination, was her ability to differentiate between the experience of *letting it happen* in contrast to *doing it*. She wrote:

An early discovery in class or private work is that will-power and effort impede movement. Gritting the teeth and trying inhibits the feel of the movement quality .... Whether it is a given exercise, or free improvisation, one has to learn to *let it happen* as contrasted to *doing* it .... The ego learns slowly an attitude toward what *wants* moving .... Movement, to be experienced, has to be *found* in the body, not put on like a dress or a coat.

A woman describes this experience: 'Once, the first time I experienced "being moved" rather than moving, I was sitting quietly cross-legged on the floor with my eyes shut. Mary had said that we should rise in the simplest, most direct way we could without overtones. I had only been working in her classes for about six months and I had absolutely no muscle control or technical ability but I rose in one complete corkscrew. Physically, if I had been asked to do it, I could not have. IT moved me, I did nothing. It impressed me more than I can say – in retrospect it seems to have been the beginning (despite a

27

couple of years of analysis) of a new understanding of the autonomy of inner images.'

(Whitehouse 1963, pp. 4–6)

Mary helped her students understand the difference between movement that is directed by the ego ('I am moving') and movement that comes from the unconscious ('I am being moved'). She spoke of the difficulties that can occur when an individual's experience is extremely one-sided. For example, some people are cut off from the unconscious. They are happiest doing planned, structured exercises. 'I move' is all they know. At the other end, there are those who live their lives in an unconscious haze. These people may be able to improvise, but it looks vague, curiously disembodied, as if no one is doing it, but it's happening by itself. The experience of 'being moved' is all they know (Whitehouse 1958, pp. 11–13). She emphasized the need to develop *both* ways. She understood that the creative process must include both conscious and unconscious.

The core of the movement experience is the sensation of moving and being moved. There are many implications in putting it like this. Ideally, both are present in the same instant and it may literally be an instant. It is a moment of total awareness, the coming together of what I am doing and what is happening to me. It cannot be anticipated, explained, specifically worked for, nor repeated exactly.

(Whitehouse 1958, p. 4)

In one of her lectures, she discussed the origins of the movement impulse:

Where does movement come from? It originates in ... a specific inner impulse having the quality of sensation. This impulse leads outward into space so that movement becomes visible as physical action. Following the inner sensation, allowing the impulse to take the form of physical action is active imagination in movement, just as following the visual image is active imagination in phantasy. It is here that the most dramatic psychophysical connections are made available to consciousness.

(Whitehouse 1963, p. 3)

Opening the channel between inner sensation and physical

action is the essential first step. With that connection, imaginative experiences present themselves 'in the manner of dreams, vivid, ephemeral, full of affect' (Whitehouse 1963, p. 6). Sometimes the movement would be accompanied by visual images, such as the spontaneous appearance of an inner landscape or inner figures. Sometimes people would remember long-forgotten dreams, or there would be a sudden rush of emotions connected with past events (Whitehouse 1963, p. 9). She also encouraged people to move their dreams and fantasies. In an interview with Gilda Frantz, she emphasized the importance of staying with the image:

'When the image is truly connected in certain people then the movement is authentic. There is no padding of movement just for the sake of moving. There is an ability to stand the inner tension until the next image moves them. They don't simply dance around.'

(Whitehouse, in Frantz 1972, p. 41)

In her classes during the structured warm-up exercises, Mary usually faced her students or clients. Eyes were generally open as everyone moved more or less in unison. Then when it was time to begin a period of inner listening, she would tell people to find their own place in the room, go inside, and wait for an impulse or image to move them. At this point of transition, she withdrew to a corner of the room to watch. The experience of the movers was contained by Mary's attentive yet non-intrusive presence. She often said that the process of Jungian analysis had been essential for her and that it was her own experience of the unconscious that in some way enabled her students to work deeply. She felt that a therapist who wanted to do this kind of work must develop the kind of ongoing, continuing relationship to the unconscious that is central to the analytic process. Lack of depth in the witness will limit the experience of the mover. Yet Mary gave only minimal attention to understanding the subtle and complex relationship between mover and witness. Her primary interest was to explore and understand the inner experience of the mover. A number of her students and others have been building on the foundation of her work, toward a deeper understanding of the inner experience of the witness and the relationship between mover and witness (Adler, Avstreih, Bernstein, Chodorow, Dosamantes-Alperson, Fay and Wyman).

Chapter Four

DANCE THERAPY TO ANALYSIS

OTHER DANCE THERAPY INFLUENCES

Marian Chace was a Denishawn dancer and teacher who, over a period of years, began to recognize that her way of working with people had therapeutic as well as aesthetic value. In the early 1940s, she was invited to work with patients at Saint Elizabeth's, the large federal psychiatric hospital in the Washington DC area. She was also the first dance therapist at Chestnut Lodge, where she was influenced by the work of Frieda Fromm-Reichmann and Harry Stack Sullivan. Marian Chace developed an approach to dance therapy that emphasizes communication of feelings in the context of group interaction:

> His meaningful, though bizarre movements become understandable and acceptable to others as people relate themselves to him on the basis of the emotions expressed through dance action. As his feeling of isolation and his fear of a lack of understanding are reduced, he is able to put aside autistic expression to an increasing degree, and this in turn seems to enable him to enter a group and function within it in a manner that is satisfying both to the patient himself, and to others in the group.
>
> (Chace 1953, p. 225)

Chace worked mainly in groups. She used phonograph music to reflect, introduce and develop different moods.

> Music selections throughout the session are consonant with the prevailing emotional tone of the group. A group in which depression predominates will start with slow waltzes and progress through lively waltzes to polkas or square dance music

and return to a lively waltz. With a group of excited patients, the session starts by moving to loud, lively music and ends with listening to contemplative music such as a Bach suite or a Debussy prelude.

(Chace 1953, p. 221)

As leader she picked up movement themes from individual patients and incorporated them into her own body. Often talking while she danced, she would echo some of the words and phrases uttered by her patients, enlarging and rhythmically transforming both verbalization and physical action. She also encouraged patients to take turns leading the group, 'passing leadership back and forth from members of the group to the dance therapist and her assistants' (Chace 1975, p. 76).

It was out of such groups that a series of dance-dramas were conceived. These were written, choreographed, produced, rehearsed and performed by the patients. The first, 'Hotel Saint Elizabeth's,' was a satire on life in the hospital. The next production, 'Cry of Humanity' was a three-hour long, spellbinding interpretation of the life of Dorothea Dix and the problems of the mentally ill. Involvement in these and other dance-drama productions offered many patients their first experience of successful participation in a vital, creative community.

Irmgard Bartenieff was another pioneer dance therapist. She was born in Germany at the turn of the century. Her background in biology, art and dance came together through her studies with Rudolf Laban. Laban was an extraordinarily innovative, charismatic Austrian who participated in the major European artistic activities of his time, especially the development of modern dance. He is the originator of Labananalysis, a subtle and complex system of movement observation, analysis and notation. Labananalysis includes: Labanotation (which notates the quantitative aspects of body movement), Effort/Shape (which notates its qualitative aspects), and Space Harmony (which addresses the body's relationship to space, utilizing the axes, planes, points and surfaces of various polyhedral forms – as if the mover were at the center of a cube, or octahedron, or icosahedron).

In 1936 Irmgard fled Nazi Germany and came to America, where she became a physical therapist. Combining Laban's movement principles with anatomical and neurological concepts, she developed a series of corrective exercises for patients in the polio wards. Since then, her 'correctives' have evolved into 'Bartenieff

Fundamentals,' a highly differentiated approach to developing and understanding the three-dimensional, full-range potential of human body movement. In addition to teaching her Fundamentals, she taught all other aspects of Labananalysis to dancers, choreographers and movement educators, as well as dance therapists, physical therapists, psychologists and anthropologists. In addition to her practice and teaching, she engaged in ongoing research that included a study of small-group behavior and a study of the individual movement patterns of psychiatric patients. She was also involved in cross-cultural studies of human movement patterns, studies of mother–infant relationships and studies of animal behavior.

During the years that I was developing my own way of working, I drew from my studies with Trudi Schoop and Mary Whitehouse, as well as from additional years of study and collaboration with Irmgard Bartenieff. I became aware of the contribution of Marian Chace through correspondence with her, getting to know her students and reading her papers. Images of all four women seemed to play through me, particularly as I led groups.

As a young dance therapist, I was puzzled by theory, but also curious about it. On one hand, the healing power of dance was self-evident. On the other hand, as my colleagues and I sought to establish our fledgeling profession, there was constant discussion about the need to develop our own theoretical framework.

I met Dr Alma Hawkins in 1971 at an east coast conference of the American Dance Therapy Association. She had established the Dance Department at UCLA and was now developing their dance therapy graduate program. We each presented something of our work at the conference and recognized many similarities. She showed a film of her work with patients (Hawkins 1972). A rich dialogue emerged in a general session and continued between us on the plane ride back to California. Her good questions got me thinking more about the nature of the imagination and how it relates to the theoretical underpinnings of dance therapy. A group of us formed a small, leaderless 'theory study group' that met regularly at her home for several years. We read everything we could about the relationship of the body, the imagination, and consciousness. We exchanged ideas, developed concepts and found various ways to put our ideas together. Our reading and discussions helped us develop a common vocabulary.

We devised a number of theoretical models and organized conferences around them. Presenters were asked to relate their work to the aspects or components of dance therapy that we identified. One model (Govine *et al.* 1973) distinguished four theoretical levels of development: 1) *awareness* of the body; 2) *range of response*, i.e., extending movement vocabulary; 3) *authentic response*; 4) *integration* of movement and meaning. Another model (Hawkins *et al.* 1980) identified five aspects of dance therapy practice: 1) interactive process; 2) bodily felt sense; 3) use of imagery; 4) therapeutic relationship; and 5) verbalization. These were not offered as finished models. Rather, they were offered as points of reference to clarify each therapist's approach and encourage a continuing process of conceptual development.

PSYCHOANALYTIC INFLUENCES

In addition to the work of the dance therapy pioneers, there were other important contributions to the development of the field. Psychoanalytic influences naturally include the work of the depth psychology pioneers, Freud, Adler, Jung and Rank. But the contributions of Reich, Sullivan and Jung are particularly recognized, because the issues they focus on are fundamental to dance therapy practice (Schmais 1974, p. 9).

Wilhelm Reich is a major influence because of his attention to the expressive language of the body. His understanding of 'defensive armour,' i.e., repressed emotion that gets stored in the body as chronic muscular tension, and his belief in the value of cathartic release has been essential to the work of many dance therapists.

Sullivan's interpersonal theory of personality has also been important to the development of the field. Chace, her students and many others see dance therapy primarily as an interactive group process. People reflect and mirror each other's movements and/or, they develop a movement-based dialogue that interweaves different qualities. Marian Chace describes something of this:

The movements used in establishing initial contact with a patient may be qualitatively similar to those of the patient (not an exact mimicking, since this is often construed by the patient as mocking) or they may be expressive of an entirely different emotion with which the therapist has responded to the patient's gestures.

(Chace 1953, p. 221)

C.G. Jung's understanding of the therapeutic value of artistic experience is essential to the theory and practice of dance therapy as well as all of the other creative art therapies. Claire Schmais writes:

> Jung's work gave credence to the use of art as a means by which the patient could become an object to himself. He viewed the artistic experience, or what he called 'active imagination,' as having both a diagnostic and therapeutic function. The creative act evokes material that is available for analysis and is at the same time cathartic. By virtue of the nonliteral or apparently nonrational aspects of the creative act, deep feelings that defy words can be symbolically represented.
>
> (Schmais 1974, p. 9)

In a broad sense, active imagination is Jung's analytical method of psychotherapy. It involves opening to the unconscious and giving free rein to fantasy, while at the same time maintaining a conscious viewpoint. In addition to his method, Jungian thought offers a vast theoretical foundation from which others have built and continue to build. This book will attempt to extend these developments, from the perspective of dance, movement and the body experience.

TOWARD DANCE/MOVEMENT AS ACTIVE IMAGINATION

As a young dance therapist, I worked in a number of clinical settings that offered a wealth of experience with people of all ages who were in treatment for every kind of psychiatric syndrome. When working with psychotic people and others who seemed to be overwhelmed by the unconscious, I found myself using dance and movement first to make contact, and then to build toward a more embodied, conscious experience of ourselves, each other and the world. When working in this way, I tended to set definite goals. I felt it was my job to bring attention and life to 'dead'-looking parts of peoples' bodies and to help each person extend their range of movement possibilities. Such structured sessions often included studies of basic rhythms, breathing exercises, ballet and contemporary dance techniques and a wide variety of ethnic dance forms, as well as playful interactions and every form of dance improvisation.

When working with people who function relatively well in the everyday world, but feel cut off from their inner resources, I tend to use much less structure and turn to the body itself as guide to the unconscious. To illustrate this, I remember a young woman who arrived for her hour one day in a hyperactive, uncomfortable mood. I asked her simply to allow herself to be or move in any way she felt. We used no music. She started moving many different ways, but it was disjointed and chaotic. Something would start and then it would seem to get cut off. Then something else would start. But nothing came together – she just looked increasingly irritable and at odds with herself. But gradually, as she became more conscious of feeling pressure and frustration, a form began to emerge. She began to move with clarity and purpose, creating a space for herself. Her movement began spontaneously to integrate with her breathing and she began to attend to the moment-to-moment process of what her body was doing. At the very end, she was sitting on the floor, legs folded, spine easily stretched upwards, as she made smaller and smaller circles with the top of her head, using the base of her spine as a fulcrum. These last movements were very subtle and centered; she was breathing easily and looked peaceful and grounded. When she opened her eyes, she had a string of insights that included a realization that her hyperactive mood had been a mask of avoidance. From the movement experience, she realized that she had been feeling pressured and restricted by certain people in her life. When she was able to let herself feel the terrible frustration, she could identify the problem and begin to do something about it. Her imaginative solution was to become more definite and assertive with herself and others – to metaphorically claim her own space. The self-directed movement process also reflected an archetypal theme. It took her through chaos to a new sense of order.

There is another woman I remember who for the first time expressed in dance/movement a prevailing mood in her life. She described the mood as 'slow and depressed and dreary.' We chose a piece of music that would reflect something of these feelings: the final theme of the score by Ravi Shankar from the film *Charly*. At first she lay on the ground, waiting, listening to the music. When she started to move, it looked as if everything she did was an overwhelming effort, as if each of her arms, legs, head and trunk weighed hundreds of pounds. By allowing herself to express symbolically the 'dead weight' of depression, she was led to experience its emotional core. The feeling was of profound sadness, helplessness and resignation. She was deeply involved in the experience and was able to stay with it. As the music came to an end she began to sob softly and deeply.

Through the years I have found myself drawn increasingly to such an inner directed way of working. To engage in this work, the mover needs to develop the capacity to bear a certain quality of tension. The opposites of conscious and unconscious have to be constellated and somehow contained. Although it is most often useful for individuals who have already developed a strong conscious viewpoint, I have at times found it to be beneficial to people in the midst of a psychosis. In this way of working, the therapist's role is not so much to structure, motivate or overtly interact, rather it is to be emotionally present, while at the same time maintaining a conscious, reflective viewpoint. This shift first led me to become a psychotherapist, then seek analytic training and eventually practice as a Jungian analyst.

Throughout this period of change and development, I remained immersed in questions about how to bridge the verbal and non-verbal aspects of psychotherapy. It was clear to me as well as to other dance therapists that a self-directed, imaginative movement process takes people directly to the deepest affects. But then, once we're there, the question comes: What do we do with it? I remember many searching discussions with colleagues about this. On one hand, we knew there is value to emotional catharsis. It releases tension and most people feel better afterwards. Also, it can reverse a process of denial and repression and help people experience themselves and relate to others with depth and authenticity. But, on the other hand, cathartic expression alone doesn't necessarily lead to psychological integration. There are situations when people simply get to be good at crying or shouting and it becomes a defense against genuine feeling and relationship.

Both of the women I have just described were able to move to and through the most intense emotional onslaughts. Each emerged with spontaneous insight and new integration. Such a deep, inner-directed process has its own life and timing. When it is like this, I have usually had enough sense to get out of the way, let the spontaneous process do its work, and feel grateful. But there are other times when a powerful flood of emotion interrupts the symbolic process. When this happens, the mover may detach from the experience with a rigid, brittle or even dissociated quality. Or, the mover may be engulfed by the affect and remain identified with it for some time.

For years I fostered cathartic release over suppression as if they were the only choices. But gradually, the image of containment became clear as a third option. To contain the affect is not to suppress or deny it. And it's not to get rid of it through a cathartic purge. To contain is to feel deeply what is in us, bear the terrible discomfort, and find a way to express it symbolically. Symbolic expression holds the tension of the opposites. We feel the full impact while at the same time maintaining a bit of observing ego. Development occurs when we contain the affect; the therapeutic relationship is at once container and process. The image of the container, the alchemical *temenos* was central to my decision to go into psychoanalytic training.

As I look back over my early experiences in dance and dance therapy, it's a continual source of interest to realize that what I was seeing and doing and recognizing only intuitively has now become conscious in a new way and is increasingly differentiated by my greater understanding of theoretical underpinnings. I also see my studies with Carmelita Maracci, Trudi Schoop, and Mary Whitehouse, as well as the years of working with children, from a new perspective. These vivid, emotional, creative experiences offered the soundest possible psychological foundation for subsequent training in traditional psychotherapy, psychoanalysis and practice as a Jungian analyst.

Nowadays programs for the training of dance therapists are able to provide concurrent psychological training in greater depth than was available in the very early days. This fosters an integration of dance therapy with the broad psychotherapy community. If there is any part of my early experience that I would most highly recommend, it is that from the beginning, training in dance therapy as well as all forms of psychotherapy and analysis would profit greatly from work with children and with patients who are in treatment for all types of emotional disorders in clinics and hospitals.

Just as dance therapy is deepened and enriched by psychological training, the training of traditional psychotherapists and psychoanalysts is deepened and enriched by training in dance/movement, particularly dance therapy. It is important to remember that the earliest experience we have of consciousness is through the body. Physical consciousness is the foundation from which we continue to develop psychologically. In a recent essay, Judith Hubback reflects on the psychological benefit of being grounded in the body: 'Patients who live well in their bodies produce images which develop into symbols much more readily than those who do not appreciate themselves as physical beings' (1988, p. 26).

I have told something of my own story to show in an immediate way how dance/movement is of value to psychotherapy, particularly as a form of active imagination. In the next section I will present a theory of depth psychology that reflects, supports and differentiates my understanding of expressive movement. It is based on the emotions, their modes of expression and their role in psychological development.

DEPTH PSYCHOLOGY AND THE EMOTIONS

INTRODUCTION TO PART TWO

In seeking a theoretical framework for any form of active imagination, one is naturally led to the psychology of C.G. Jung. Active imagination is an approach that Jung developed out of his own need to discover the meaning of dreams and fantasy images, as well as the meaning of autonomous emotional complexes that erupt in ordinary life and in the therapeutic relationship. As a technique for bringing unconscious contents to consciousness, active imagination can be done in any number of ways, according to the individual's taste and talent. As early as 1916, Jung wrote about some of his patients who used body movement to give form to the unconscious. But despite Jung's interest in dance/movement as a form of active imagination, its role in Jungian thought and practice has remained largely undeveloped.

We shall approach Jungian thought from the perspective of two themes that I believe are essential to understanding dance/movement as a form of active imagination. These are, 1) the body-psyche relationship, and 2) the affects (i.e. emotions). The first theme leads to the next, because it is the affects that function as the bridge between body and psyche.

As described at length in the first section of this book, it is clear that emotion and dance are inseparable. Dance is motivated by and expressive of emotion. Emotion is the source out of which we dance, i.e. it energizes us. But dance also has an effect on our emotions. It changes them. Sometimes dance leads to cathartic release; other times, dance seems to develop, refine and completely transform our emotional state.

Dance therapy too, is about the body-psyche relationship and the affects. Whether working with a psychotic child who seems to live in a tiny, intense world of stylized emotional expression – or with a psychotic or neurotic adult whose body may reflect years of

41

repressed or undeveloped emotional life; the dance therapist utilizes dance/movement and body experience toward the expression, communication and transformation of emotion.

Every form of psychotherapy (including dance therapy) is involved with the diagnosis and treatment of emotional dysfunction. Whether approaching the therapeutic relationship from the perspective of behavior, insight or depth psychology, emotion is a central concern of every psychotherapy and every analysis.

For Jung, the emotions are the foundation of the psyche. They are the source of psychic energy. Our most troublesome complexes are formed around an emotional core. At the same time, the emotions are the origin of our highest values.

For the past several years, Louis H. Stewart has been updating Jung's model of the psyche in light of recent studies of the emotions and their universal forms of expression. Following Jung, he understands the affects to be central to the development of consciousness, as well as being the bridge between body and psyche. Building on the seminal research of Silvan Tomkins, Stewart proposes a limited number of innate affects. These function as the energic and transformative matrix out of which the world of everyday feelings and emotional complexes is developed. The primal, innate affects are modulated and transformed in the crucible of the family. Play and the imagination are fundamental to this process.

Stewart's contribution is central to our topic. We shall review his hypothesis as to the nature of the affects, individually and as a system, and the relationship of the affects to other functions of the psyche. I have found this material to be essential to a more differentiated understanding of the origins of the movement impulse, the meaning of the symbolic actions, images, and the whole transformative process. He is building on the work of Jung, Henderson's concept of the cultural layer of the unconscious and the cultural attitudes, Hillman's study on the phenomenology and meaning of emotion, Neumann's contribution to development, as well as the work of other Jungian authors. In addition to Tomkins' original research on the affects, he draws from Ekman, Izard and others who have been building on the foundation of Tomkins' work. Additional source material includes Roberts and Sutton-Smith on anthropological research about play and games, and richly detailed observations of infants and children by Piaget. Philosophical sources include contributions from the work of Bachelard, Cassirer and Kant.

We shall begin with Jung's comments on the body-psyche relationship. This will lead to Jung's early studies and continuing thought on the nature of the affects. As we turn to the structure of the psyche, the dynamics of the psyche and psychological development, we shall review much of Stewart's source material and explore his synthesis.

Chapter Five

JUNG ON BODY, PSYCHE, EMOTION

BODY AND PSYCHE

Psyche and matter are 'two different aspects of one and the same thing' (Jung 1947, p. 215). 'It seems highly probable that the psychic and the physical are not two independent parallel processes, but are essentially connected through reciprocal action ...' (Jung 1912/1928, p. 18). What we call psychic includes both physical and spiritual dimensions (Jung 1929, p. 51). Jung envisions an analogy to the color spectrum between two poles, ranging from 'the "psychic infra-red," the biological instinctual psyche' to 'the "psychic ultra violet," the archetype ...' (Jung 1947, p. 215). He proposes the existence of a 'psychoid level' which is located in the depths of the unconscious where the two poles in some way meet. The psychoid level functions as a kind of transformative interface between psyche and matter.

Jung's interest in the body-psyche relationship seems to go back to his childhood. While still a boy, he came to the realization that he had two 'personalities.' Personality Number One was grounded in the reality of his body and the facts of the world the way it is. Personality Number Two lived in a mythic realm, eternal time, the world of the ancestors and spirits. Reflecting on this experience, he wrote:

> The play and counterplay between personalities No. 1 and No. 2, which has run through my whole life, has nothing to do with a 'split' or dissociation in the ordinary medical sense. On the contrary, it is played out in every individual.
>
> (Jung 1961a, p. 45)

The two personalities he experienced, developed into two seemingly irreconcilable areas of professional interest. On one hand, he was drawn to study the natural sciences. On the other hand, he was fascinated by ancient history, philosophy and mysticism. When he read a book by Krafft-Ebing on psychiatry, he was seized by an intense excitement and realized that his two passions could come together:

My heart suddenly began to pound. I had to stand up and draw a deep breath. My excitement was intense, for it had become clear to me in a flash of illumination, that for me the only possible goal was psychiatry. Here alone the two currents of my interest could flow together and in a united stream dig their own bed. Here was the empirical field common to biological and spiritual facts, which I had everywhere sought and nowhere found. Here at last was the place where the collision of nature and spirit became a reality.

(Jung 1961a, pp. 108–9)

As a psychiatric resident at the Burgholzli Clinic in Zurich, Jung was fascinated by the mysterious, perseverative gestures made by some of the most regressed patients (1961, pp. 124–5). One of the women patients had been mute for many years. When he noticed that she continually made certain odd movements with her hands and head, he shut his eyes and repeated her movements himself, in order to sense what she might be feeling. He spoke out loud the first words that came to him. The woman's response was to say: 'How did you know?' From that moment, a connection was made. The woman had been considered incurable, but was soon able to talk with him about her dreams and was then able to be discharged. After this, he frequently relied on the symbolic meaning of unconscious motor phenomena to understand and communicate with patients who were extremely withdrawn (Fay 1977, p. 183; Jung 1902, par. 82; Van der Post 1979).

THE NATURE OF THE AFFECTS

Jung's early word association studies attempted to measure the physiological changes that occur when a psychological complex is touched. His objective was to understand the nature of the emotionally toned complex. Jung's studies of the affective core of the complex are of special interest to our topic, because he defined the affect as having both somatic and psychic aspects. 'By the term affect I mean a state of feeling characterized by marked physical innervation on the one hand and a peculiar disturbance of the ideational process on the other' (Jung 1921, p. 411).

Jung speaks of the difference between his view and the James–Lange theory of affect. The James–Lange theory suggests that bodily innervations are causal; i.e., physical innervations cause the emotion. But Jung holds that emotion functions as a dynamic bridge – a kind of dialectical interaction between psyche and soma: 'I regard affect on the one hand as a psychic feeling-state and on the other as a physiological innervation-state, each of which has a cumulative effect on the other' (Jung 1921, pp. 412).

In an essay completed shortly before his death, Jung discusses the function of emotion in relation to the archetypal experience. An archetypal *experience* includes both image and affect. In contrast, an archetypal *image* may be 'only an image' if there is no emotional response in the one who sees it. In their original form, archetypes are

> images and at the same time emotions. One can speak of an archetype only when these two aspects coincide. When there is only an image, it is merely a word-picture, like a corpuscle with no electric charge. It is then of little consequence, just a word and nothing more. But if the image is charged with numinosity, that is, with psychic energy, then it becomes dynamic and will produce consequences. It is a great mistake in practice to treat an archetype as if it were a mere name, word, or concept. It is far more than that: it is a piece of life, an image connected with the living individual by the bridge of emotion.
>
> (Jung 1961b, p. 257)

In addition to understanding emotion as bridge between instinct and archetype, body and psyche, Jung also speaks of emotion as source of value (Jung 1951, pp. 27–8 and 32–3), imagery (Jung 1961a, p. 177), energy and new consciousness:

> Conflict engenders fire, the fire of affects and emotions, and like every other fire it has two aspects, that of combustion and that of creating light. On the one hand, emotion is the alchemical fire whose warmth brings everything into existence and whose heat burns all superfluities to ashes (*omnes superfluitates comburit*). But on the other hand, emotion is the moment when

46

steel meets flint and a spark is struck forth, for emotion is the chief source of consciousness. There is no change from darkness to light or from inertia to movement without emotion.

(Jung 1938a, p. 96)

For Jung, the emotionally toned complex is the key to understanding the unconscious processes that produce psychogenic symptoms. A complex is 'a collection of various ideas held together by an emotional tone common to all' (Jung 1911, p. 599). The complex is usually formed when circumstances evoke an emotional response that cannot be borne. That unbearable emotion or emotional tone gets split off from consciousness and an autonomous complex begins to form. The affective core of the complex gathers around itself a collection of interrelated ideas, impressions, memory traces and behavior patterns. This network of affectively interwoven associations may include not only aspects of personal history, but cultural and primordial themes as well.

The problematic aspect of the complex has to do with its autonomy. Although we may reject, deny and even structure our lives to avoid its emotional content, it remains active. The complex doesn't go away. Instead, it lives on in the unconscious, i.e. outside the control of the conscious mind. Emotionally toned complexes usually make themselves known through unconscious states of projection and possession, which often have a driven, compulsive, fanatic or even demonic quality. Complexes appear in dreams and visions, as well as in mental disturbances. Complexes may convert and manifest as somatic symptoms. The phenomenon of ghosts and spirits, too, may be understood psychologically as projections of autonomous complexes.

When we are in a complex, its affective core engulfs us with its characteristic emotional tone or mood. It may compel us to think unwanted thoughts (that we may not even agree with) and act out in troublesome ways. 'Everyone knows nowadays that people "have complexes." What is not so well known, though far more important theoretically, is that complexes can *have us*' (Jung 1934a, p. 96).

When Jung read *The Interpretation of Dreams* in 1903, he recognized that Freud's concept of repression was applicable to his own work with the emotionally toned complex:

I had frequently encountered repressions in my experiments with word association; in response to certain stimulus words the patient either had no associative answer or was unduly slow in his reaction time. As was later discovered, such a disturbance occurred each time the stimulus word had touched upon a psychic lesion or conflict. In most cases the patient was unconscious of this. When questioned about the cause of the disturbance, he would often answer in a peculiarly artificial manner. My reading of Freud's *The Interpretation of Dreams* showed me that the repression mechanism was at work here, and that the facts I had observed were consonant with his theory. Thus I was able to corroborate Freud's line of argument.

(Jung 1961a, p. 147)

Although Jung agreed with Freud about the psychological mechanism of repression, they had different views about the content of repression. For Freud, sexual trauma was the root cause of repression. Jung knew that sexual trauma was sometimes the cause, but he was also familiar with numerous cases of neurosis in which sexuality played a background role. Jung held that emotional trauma could occur in relation to any number of difficult or tragic factors that influence the life of an individual.

This difference was also reflected in their views about the nature of libido. During the years of his association with Jung, Freud believed that libido was exclusively sexual; he saw sexual energy and its sublimation as the source of all human motivation and culture. Jung on the other hand, had reservations about such a narrow definition and proposed a much broader, more inclusive concept of psychic energy. For Jung, libido is a dynamic, energic, transformative function. Its ontogenetic origins can be traced to the infant's rhythmic expression of primal drives and affects. It is basically creative energy.

As we reflect on Jung's understanding of the nature of the psyche, it may be helpful to remember that he was an empiricist. His psychology is based on simple, direct observation of human experience. Affect, archetype, complex and libido are at once concepts and palpable experiences.

Chapter Six

THE STRUCTURE OF THE UNCONSCIOUS

In his memoirs, Jung reports a dream that eventually led him to develop the concept of the collective unconscious:

> I was in a house I did not know, which had two stories. It was 'my house.' I found myself in the upper story, where there was a kind of salon furnished with fine old pieces in rococo style. On the walls hung a number of precious old paintings. I wondered that this should be my house, and thought 'Not bad.' But then it occurred to me that I did not know what the lower floor looked like. Descending the stairs, I reached the ground floor. There everything was much older, and I realized that this part of the house must date from about the fifteenth or sixteenth century. The furnishings were medieval; the floors were of red brick. Everywhere it was rather dark. I went from one room to another thinking, 'Now I really must explore the whole house.' I came upon a heavy door, and opened it. Beyond it, I discovered a stone stairway that led down into the cellar. Descending again, I found myself in a beautifully vaulted room which looked exceedingly ancient. Examining the walls, I discovered layers of brick among the ordinary stone blocks, and chips of brick in the mortar. As soon as I saw this I knew that the walls dated from Roman times. My interest by now was intense. I looked more closely at the floor. It was of stone slabs, and in one of these I discovered a ring. When I pulled it, the stone slab lifted, and again I saw a stairway of narrow stone steps leading down into the depths. These, too, I descended, and entered a low cave cut into the rock. Thick dust lay on the floor, and in the dust were scattered bones and broken pottery, like remains of a primitive culture. I discovered two human skulls, obviously very old and half disintegrated. Then I awoke.
>
> (Jung 1961a, p. 158–9)

During the days before this dream, Jung had been thinking about psychoanalytic theory, particularly Freud's view that the unconscious is made up of repressed personal history. Obviously Jung agreed that psychic contents that have been repressed are part of the unconscious. But he wondered whether there might be more. The dream seemed to speak to his questions. To Jung, it was clear that the house represented an image of the structure of the psyche.

His own state of consciousness was represented by the inhabited first-story salon. Its style was drawn from the historical atmosphere of Basel at the end of the nineteenth century – an image of the world in which Jung had lived during his formative years. The uninhabited ground floor represented the first level of the unconscious. After that, the deeper he went, the darker and more alien the scene became. The Roman cellar and the prehistoric cave represented successive layers in the history of consciousness.

> My dream thus constituted a kind of structural diagram of the human psyche; it postulated something of an altogether *impersonal* nature underlying that psyche .... It was my first inkling of a collective a priori beneath the personal psyche.
>
> (Jung 1961a, p. 161)

Jung's dream of the house revived his old interest in archaeology. From reading about Babylonian excavations, his interest turned to ancient mythology. As his ideas clarified, a book entitled *Symbols of Transformation* began to take form. Jung knew that his book would mark the divergence of his own ideas from those of Freud. In addition to holding different views on the content of repression and the nature of the libido, Jung and Freud had come to a different understanding about the nature of the unconscious. In contrast to Freud's emphasis on the unconscious as repressed personal history, Jung increasingly understood it to include both personal and collective history. Below consciousness, there lies the first or personal layer of the unconscious. Underneath that lie the foundations of cultural history and underneath that, the primordial depths. These are innate functions that have evolved through the ages and are shared by all humankind. Jung and Freud were unable to reconcile their differences. In addition to the issues discussed here, there were other major issues that go beyond the scope of this study. Their collaboration and friendship came to an end in 1913 after the publication of Jung's book.

Following the break with Freud, Jung went through a difficult period of inner uncertainty and disorientation, which led him to undertake a deep process of psychological development. It was out of his own confrontation with the unconscious that he developed the method of active imagination. During the years 1913–1919 he published very little. But the major works of his life were incubating. When he emerged from these years of relative retreat, he was ready to take on the leadership of his own school of psychology.

In a 1920 paper, Jung offers a richly detailed statement about the nature of the unconscious. Here he differentiates the *contents* of the personal unconscious from the *functions* of the collective unconscious. The contents of the personal unconscious are acquired. The functions of the unconscious, that is to say the organizing principles of the psyche – are inherited.

According to my view, the unconscious falls into two parts which should be sharply distinguished from one another. One of them is the personal unconscious; it includes all those psychic contents which have been forgotten during the course of the individual's life. Traces of them are still preserved in the unconscious, even if all conscious memory of them has been lost. In addition, it contains all subliminal impressions or perceptions which have too little energy to reach consciousness. To these we must add unconscious combinations of ideas that are still too feeble and too indistinct to cross over the threshold. Finally, the personal unconscious contains all psychic contents that are incompatible with the conscious attitude. This comprises a whole group of contents, chiefly those which appear morally, aesthetically, or intellectually inadmissible and are repressed on account of their incompatibility. A man cannot always think and feel the good, the true, and the beautiful, and in trying to keep up an ideal attitude everything that does not fit in with it is automatically repressed .... The other part of the unconscious is what I call the impersonal or collective unconscious. As the name indicates, its contents are not personal but collective; that is, they do not belong to one individual alone but to a whole group of individuals, and generally to a whole nation, or even to the whole of mankind. These contents are not acquired during the individual's lifetime but are products of innate forms and instincts. Although the child possesses no inborn ideas, it nevertheless has a highly developed brain which functions in a

51

quite definite way. This brain is inherited from its ancestors; it is the deposit of the psychic functioning of the whole human race. The child therefore brings with it an organ ready to function in the same way as it has functioned throughout human history. In the brain the instincts are preformed, and so are the primordial images which have always been the basis of man's thinking – the whole treasure-house of mythological motifs.*

(Jung 1920, pp. 310–11)

Jung adds a very important footnote:

* By this I do not mean the existing form of the motif but its preconscious, invisible 'ground plan.' This might be compared to the crystal lattice which is preformed in the crystalline solution. It should not be confused with the variously structured axial system of the individual crystal.

(Jung 1920, p. 311)

The lattice in a crystalline solution holds within itself an unseen yet typical pattern of development. Variously structured individual forms are crystallized out of a dialectic between the invisible 'ground plan' (i.e. the lattice) and environmental influences. One thinks here of myriad, tiny six-sided snowflakes. All are organized out of the same snow crystal lattice which shapes their development through a hexagonal tension. Yet no two are alike. Snowflakes are formed out of an interaction between their preformed lattice and such environmental influences as temperature, pressure and other atmospheric conditions. In order better to understand Jung's metaphor, we must differentiate between the innate images and instincts in their preconscious state and the rich variety of mythic images and behavior patterns that are available to consciousness.

As we consider the interweaving of innate potential with environmental influence, we are led to the cultural aspect of the unconscious. Jung assumed that the unconscious includes cultural as well as personal and universal contents (Henderson 1985/1986). But he never developed a concept specifically to address the structure and function of the cultural aspect of the unconscious.

The concept of the cultural unconscious and a theory of cultural attitudes was introduced by Joseph L. Henderson in 1962. Henderson calls for an enlargement of Jung's concept of the collective unconscious to include the cultural unconscious. The cultural unconscious has two aspects. One aspect is derived from the cultural environment through the unconscious influence of education, family life and the *Zeitgeist* or spirit of the times. The other (similar to the crystal lattice) holds within itself a potential pattern of imaginative development. When this latent function is awakened by the rich cultural atmosphere that family, education and the *Zeitgeist* may provide, there is the dynamic interweaving of innate imaginative potential with environmental influence. The activation of such a dialectic may lead to the ongoing, continuous process of symbolic development that is essential to individuation. This symbolic process may be seen as the dynamic function of the cultural unconscious.

For Henderson, the cultural layer of the unconscious is

represented by those historical remnants of which Jung speaks, but we know that these remnants could never be activated without some significant original stimulus from environment, some educational experience powerful enough to awaken these latent contents. In an illiterate, undisciplined and completely uncultivated person, we would not find any significant production from this layer. Such an educational experience ... is built up through many exposures to cultural canons of taste, of moral principles, of social custom, and of religious symbolism. And it is built upon certain influences from the family life in which an important part of these canons have been passed on from previous generations. Accordingly much of what has been called 'personal unconscious' is not personal at all but that part of the collective culture pattern transmitted through our environment before we were able to affirm its validity for ego consciousness.

(Henderson 1962, pp. 8–9)

The cultural attitudes are developed in an individual through the mediating function of the cultural unconscious. Henderson describes the four main cultural attitudes: the religious attitude, the aesthetic attitude, the philosophic attitude and the social attitude. He proposes a fifth emerging psychological attitude, which may be seen as a quintessence because it offers a new perspective on, and experience of, the other four (1962, 1977, 1984, 1985, 1985/1986, n.d.).

I can imagine a group of future analysts teaching a new appreciation of old cultural attitudes not because they set out to do this on purpose in any missionarizing spirit but because this teaching would be an inevitable result of their way of working with their patients.

(Henderson 1962, p. 14)

Up to this point in our discussion about the structure of the psyche, we have identified three basic levels of the unconscious: the personal, the cultural and the primordial. The personal unconscious is the most available to consciousness since it is made up predominantly of contents that were once conscious. The cultural unconscious is less available to consciousness, because the environmental cultural influences that activate it are drawn from the unconscious atmosphere of the family, the unconscious impressions gathered through education, and the unconscious elements of the *Zeitgeist*. The primordial unconscious consists of structures and dynamic functions that are not capable of becoming conscious. These form the 'omnipresent, unchanging, and everywhere identical *quality or substrate of the psyche per se*' (Jung 1951, p. 7). At this deepest level, we find the innate affects, instincts and images of the primal Self. Each of the levels we have described seems to be associated with a particular quality of expressive movement. The identification of movement qualities with different aspects of the psyche will be described in a later part of this book.

Chapter Seven

BASIC CONCEPTS

In the following pages we shall briefly discuss certain concepts that are fundamental to Jung's analytical psychology. These concepts are at the same time images or personifications of different psychic structures and their function(s). The concepts we shall discuss are:

1 The Shadow
2 The Syzygy: Anima and Animus
3 The Persona
4 The Ego
5 The Self

THE SHADOW

Jung describes the shadow as 'the sum of all those unpleasant qualities we like to hide, together with the insufficiently developed functions and the contents of the personal unconscious' (1917, p. 66f). Jung emphasizes that everyone has a shadow. There is a folk saying that 'the person without a shadow must be the devil in disguise.'

In dreams and fantasies, the shadow most often appears as a human figure who is the same sex as the dreamer. The shadow might resemble someone we know from our waking life, or it might be a dream-person, that is to say a person unknown in our waking life.

The following quotes by Jung address our human struggle to integrate the shadow. It is often extremely difficult to recognize in ourselves the tendency to project unwanted emotions on to others.

Although, with insight and good will, the shadow can to some extent be assimilated into the conscious personality, experience shows that there are certain features which offer the most obstinate resistance to moral control and prove almost impossible to influence. These resistances are usually bound up with *projections*, which are not recognized as such, and their recognition is a moral achievement beyond the ordinary. While some traits peculiar to the shadow can be recognized without too much difficulty as one's own personal qualities, in this case both insight and good will are unavailing because the cause of the emotion appears to lie, beyond all possibility of doubt, in the *other person*. No matter how obvious it may be to the neutral observer that it is a matter of projections, there is little hope that the subject will perceive this himself. He must be convinced that he throws a very long shadow before he is willing to withdraw his emotionally-toned projections from their object.

(1951, p. 9)

I should like to emphasize that the integration of the shadow, or the realization of the personal unconscious, marks the first stage in the analytic process.

(1951, p. 22)

Jung speaks not only of the personal shadow, but of the collective shadow as well:

It is quite within the bounds of possibility for a man to recognize the relative evil of his nature, but it is a rare and shattering experience for him to gaze into the face of absolute evil.

(1951, p. 10)

One thinks here of Hitler, who not only projected and inflicted his own and Germany's experience of humiliation on to the Jewish people and others who were not 'Aryan,' he at the same time projected and was possessed by a massive complex of all-consuming destruction and rage. The following quote is Hitler's description of Churchill:

For over five years this man has been chasing around Europe like a madman in search of something he could set on fire. Unfortunately he again and again finds hirelings who open the gates of their country to this international incendiary.

(Hitler, quoted in von Franz 1964, pp. 172–3)

Human survival may now depend on each individual's capacity to come to terms with the shadow so that it no longer be projected onto some other person, group or nation.

THE SYZYGY: ANIMA AND ANIMUS

As the shadow represents or personifies the personal unconscious, the anima (compensatory feminine image in a man) and the animus (compensatory masculine image in a woman) personify the cultural unconscious. Both aspects of the syzygy make themselves known to us through a particularly compelling quality of thoughts, attitudes, and moods. We also tend unconsciously to project their romantic and/or fascinating nature on to other persons, usually of the opposite sex. Another way they make themselves known is through dreams, visions and the fantasies of active imagination. The anima and animus appear as contrasexual figures to the dreamer. They usually have a human form, but may also be closely associated with an animal image or may even be part animal.

When the cultural unconscious is only minimally differentiated, the thoughts, attitudes and moods of the collective may speak through us in the form of meaningless generalizations, cliches, platitudes or righteous but unexamined convictions. When a person lives in a constant state of identification with the collective culture, that individual's life remains unlived. Yet the syzygy is capable of development and has another aspect in which anima and animus become more akin to soul and spirit. They offer great gifts. When the cultural unconscious is activated, a new relationship to this inner function becomes possible. In Jung's words:

> Just as the anima becomes, through integration, the Eros of consciousness, so the animus becomes a Logos; and in the same way that the anima gives relationship and relatedness to a man's consciousness, the animus gives to woman's consciousness a capacity for reflection, deliberation and self-knowledge.
>
> (1951, p. 16)

Henderson draws an analogy between the syzygy and the ancient Greek idea of a personal daimon. In their undeveloped form they are autonomous emotional complexes that can cause no end of trouble. Yet with consciousness they begin to serve as our guides toward the development of ultimate values.

We live during a late stage of the Christian era and we think daimonism is nothing but a relic of former times that may appear occasionally in fairy tales .... But in Jung's concept of the anima and animus, the feminine image in man and the masculine image in woman, the demons make a reappearance which more and more people are taking into consideration. What is not so clearly known is that these images undergo an evolution similar to the demons of old. Undifferentiated, seductive and unreliable, they exert a dubious effect, to say the least. But if we work patiently at making conscious the messages they bring us from the archetypal underworld, perhaps they will grow up and become the guardian spirits of old brought up to date. Thenceforth, as for the ancient Greeks they become mediators between the archetypes and the ego by way of the cultural unconscious.

(Henderson n.d., manuscript p. 22)

THE PERSONA

Jung described the persona as 'a complicated system of relations between the individual consciousness and society, fittingly enough a kind of mask, designed on one hand to make a definite impression upon others, and, on the other, to conceal the true nature of the individual' (1928a, p. 192). As anima and animus mediate between individual consciousness (i.e. ego) and the depths of the psyche, the persona mediates between the ego and the external world. Both anima/animus and the persona are made up of the cultural collective and seem to function as counterparts to each other.

The persona, like the shadow, usually personifies as a same sex human, but whereas the shadow tends to represent our less desirable characteristics, the persona tends to be more of an ego ideal. In dreams the persona might also be represented as a mask, or clothes, or the front yard, or façade of a home or building, or even a particular style of decoration.

The persona can be problematic when an individual is completely identified with a professional or social role. Such a one-sided state creates an artificial personality that lacks depth.

Similar to our task regarding the shadow and the syzygy, it is important to develop awareness of the persona. With recognition, it can be integrated into consciousness. Most of us do best with a persona that is flexible, natural and at the same time strong enough to give us comfortable boundaries. An insufficiently developed persona leaves us too vulnerable – too raw. One needs a well developed persona to have a sense of self-containment and a bit of privacy.

THE EGO

The ego is the conscious aspect of the total personality. It is through the ego (in its relation to the unconscious and the world) that we gain our sense of identity and capacity for self-reflective consciousness.

As a young man, Jung had the following dream that emphasized for him the importance of consciousness:

> It was night in some unknown place, and I was making slow and painful headway against a mighty wind. Dense fog was flying along everywhere. I had my hands cupped around a tiny light which threatened to go out at any moment. Everything depended on my keeping this little light alive. Suddenly I had the feeling that something was coming up behind me. I looked back and saw a gigantic black figure following me. But at the same moment, I was conscious, in spite of my terror, that I must keep my little light going through night and wind, regardless of all dangers.
>
> (1961a, p. 87–8)

When Jung awoke, he realized that the frightening figure was his own shadow, brought into being by the ghost-like reflection cast by his light. He knew too, that the little light he carried represented his consciousness:

> My own understanding is the sole treasure I possess, and the greatest. Though infinitely small and fragile in comparison with the powers of darkness, it is still a light, my only light.
>
> (1961a, p. 88)

In the Tavistock Lectures (1935) Jung presents a more formal definition of the nature of ego consciousness. Here he emphasizes its development from the perspective of the body and memory:

> The important fact about consciousness is that nothing can be conscious without an ego to which it refers. If something is not

related to the ego then it is not conscious. Therefore you can define consciousness as a relation of psychic facts to the ego. What is that ego? The ego is a complex datum which is constituted first of all by a general awareness of your body, of your existence, and secondly by your memory data; you have a certain idea of having been, a long series of memories. Those two are the main constituents of what we call the ego.

(1935, p. 11)

In dreams the ego usually appears as an embodied image of ourself. We speak of this figure as the dream ego. But even when dreams lack a dream ego figure, there remains a conscious viewpoint, some sense of ego as unseen witness.

Active imagination is a kind of dialogue between the conscious ego viewpoint and various personifications of the unconscious. The difference between active and passive imagination has to do with ego consciousness.

The ego is drawn to interact with the contents of the unconscious. It is equally drawn to full engagement with the external world. The flow of life instinct that draws ego consciousness toward the inner world is called *introversion*. The outward flowing aspect of this is called *extraversion*. Together these enable a natural and continual fluctuation that weaves together the experience of our inner and outer worlds. Most of us tend to develop an inclination toward one more than the other. Those who are primarily concerned with inner events are called introverts; those who are primarily concerned with outer events are called extraverts. In addition to recognizing and describing introverted and extraverted attitudes, Jung developed a typology based on four psychological functions that are intrinsic to the nature of ego consciousness. These are: *thinking*, *feeling*, *sensation* and *intuition*.

THE SELF

Jung describes the Self as 'the principle and archetype of orientation and meaning' (1961a, p. 199). The Self encompasses our psychic totality, conscious and unconscious, from the primal, untransformed depths to the ultimate development of an individual. It functions as the ordering and centering process of the psyche. It is our image of wholeness, the central archetype: 'The self is not only the centre but also the whole circumference which embraces both conscious and unconscious; it is also the centre of this totality, just as the ego is the centre of consciousness' (Jung 1936a, p. 41).

The Self is symbolically represented by images that express the tension of opposites within a totality. Jung describes the development of such images in the paintings of active imagination.

The chaotic assortment of images that at first confronted me reduced itself in the course of the work to certain well-defined themes and formal elements, which repeated themselves in identical or analogous form with the most varied individuals. I mention, as the most salient characteristics, chaotic multiplicity and order; duality; the opposition of light and dark, upper and lower, right and left; the union of opposites in a third; the quaternity (square, cross); rotation (circle, sphere); and finally the centering process and a radial arrangement that usually followed some quaternary system .... The centering process is, in my experience, the never-to-be-surpassed climax of the whole development, and is characterized as such by the fact that it brings with it the greatest possible therapeutic effect.

(1947, p. 203)

The Self may personify in any number of forms that represent its quality of wholeness. Such images may include Gods and Demons, Special Humans, Animals, Fish, Insects, Vegetation, Mineral Formations and many other natural, mythic and cosmic symbols of psychic totality.

Chapter Eight

DARWIN AND TOMKINS

Darwin's *The Expression of the Emotions in Man and Animals* (1872) is the first thorough study of individual affects and their universal forms of expression. His observations were gathered over a thirty-year period. His subjects include infants and children (particularly his own), as well as adults from every walk of life and from many different cultures. He approached the study of emotional expression from the perspective of art and literature as well as muscles and the nervous system. This work continues to inform and inspire research in many fields.

Darwin (1872) addresses the innate nature of the fundamental emotions:

> That the chief expressive actions, exhibited by man and by the lower animals, are now innate or inherited – that is, have not been learnt by the individual – is admitted by every one. So little has learning or imitation to do with several of them that they are from the earliest days and throughout life quite beyond our control; for instance, the relaxing of the arteries of the skin in blushing, and the increased action of the heart in anger .... The inheritance of most of our expressive actions explains the fact that those born blind display them .... We can thus also understand the fact that the young and the old of widely different races, both with man and animals, express the same state of mind by the same movements.
>
> (pp. 350–1)

From the perspective of Jungian thought such innate patterns of behavior have their origin in the depths of the primordial unconscious.

Darwin names thirty-seven emotional states in his table of contents and many more throughout the book. As we approach this material, it will be helpful to remember that many different words are ordinarily used to describe different facets and intensities of a single affect. For example, the expressive actions of Grief include weeping, sobbing, rocking, keening, wailing, crying, mourning, lamenting; its intensity ranges from distress, through sadness, to the extreme of anguish. Such a range is true for each of the major affects.

Although he uses many synonyms and other terms, Darwin's study is primarily focused on the fundamental emotions: Grief, Joy, Anger, Fear, Contempt, Shame and Startle. All of these have typical forms of expression that are recognized by humans from widely different cultures including isolated, pre-literate cultures. The following quotes are somewhat lengthy, but I encourage the reader to take the time to remember and imagine these universal patterns of behavior, as described by Darwin.

[GRIEF] Persons suffering from excessive grief often seek relief by violent and almost frantic movements ... but when their suffering is somewhat mitigated, yet prolonged, they no longer wish for action, but remain motionless and passive, or may occasionally rock themselves to and fro. The circulation becomes languid; the face pale; the muscles flaccid; the eyelids droop; the head hangs on the contracted chest; the lips, cheeks, and lower jaw all sink downwards from their own weight. Hence all the features are lengthened; and the face of a person who hears bad news is said to fall. A party of natives in Tierra del Fuego endeavoured to explain to us that their friend ... was out of spirits, by pulling down their cheeks with both hands, so as to make their faces as long as possible .... The corners of the mouth are drawn downward, which is so universally recognized as a sign of being out of spirits, that it is almost proverbial.

(Darwin 1872, pp. 177–8)

JOY, when intense, leads to various purposeless movements – to dancing about, clapping the hands, stamping, etc., and to loud laughter. Laughter seems primarily to be the expression of mere joy or happiness .... Laura Bridgman, from her blindness and deafness, could not have acquired any expression through imitation, yet when a letter from a beloved friend was communicated to her by gesture-language, she 'laughed and clapped her hands, and the colours mounted to her cheeks.' On other occasions she has been seen to stamp for joy.

(ibid., p. 196)

[ANGER] The excited brain gives strength to the muscles, and at the same time energy to the will. The body is commonly held erect ready for instant action, but sometimes it is bent forward towards the offending person, with the limbs more or less rigid. The mouth is generally closed with firmness, showing fixed determination, and the teeth are clenched or ground together. Such gestures as the raising of the arms, with the fists clenched, as if to strike the offender, are common .... The desire, indeed, to strike often becomes so intolerably strong, that inanimate objects are struck or dashed to the ground; but the gestures frequently become altogether purposeless or frantic. Young children, when in a violent rage roll on the ground on their backs or bellies, screaming, kicking, scratching, or biting everything within reach. So it is, as I hear from Mr. Scott, with Hindoo children; and, as we have seen, with the young of the anthropomorphous apes.

(ibid, pp. 239–40)

[FEAR] was expressed from an extremely remote period, in almost the same manner as it now is by man; namely by trembling, the erection of the hair, cold perspiration, pallor, widely opened eyes, the relaxation of most of the muscles, and by the whole body cowering downwards or held motionless.

(ibid, pp. 360–1)

Of vague fear there is a well-known and grand description in Job: 'In thoughts from the visions of the night, when deep sleep falleth on men, fear came upon me, and trembling, which made all my bones to shake. Then a spirit passed before my face; the hair of my flesh stood up. It stood still, but I could not discern the form thereof: an image was before my eyes, there was silence, and I heard a voice, saying, Shall mortal man be more just than God? Shall a man be more pure than his Maker?' (Job iv. 13.).

(ibid, p. 291)

[CONTEMPT] The most common method of expressing contempt is by movements about the nose, or round the mouth; but the latter movements, when strongly pronounced, indicate disgust. The nose may be slightly turned up, which apparently follows from the turning up of the upper lip; or the movement may be abbreviated into the mere wrinkling of the nose (pp. 254–5) .... Spitting seems an almost universal sign of contempt or disgust; and spitting obviously represents the rejection of anything offensive from the mouth.

(ibid, p. 160)

[SHAME] Under a keen sense of shame there is a strong desire for concealment. We turn away the whole body, more especially the face, which we endeavour in some manner to hide. An ashamed person can hardly endure to meet the gaze of those present, so that he invariably casts down his eyes or looks askant.

(ibid, pp. 320–1)

[STARTLE] The eyes and mouth being widely open is an expression universally recognized as one of surprise or astonishment .... That the eyebrows are raised by an innate or instinctive impulse may be inferred from the fact that Laura Bridgman invariably acts thus when astonished .... The cause of the mouth being opened when astonishment is felt, is a much more complex affair ... when we wish to listen intently to any sound, we either stop breathing, or breathe as quietly as possible, by opening our mouths, at the same time keeping our bodies motionless. One of my sons was awakened in the night by a noise under circumstances which naturally led to great care, and after a few minutes he perceived that his mouth was widely open. He then became conscious that he had opened it for the sake of breathing as quietly as possible.

(ibid, pp. 278–83)

In addition to the fundamental emotions which are innate, Darwin differentiates the complex emotions. Complex emotions are known to humans in every culture, but they lack prototypical patterns of behavior. Some of the complex emotions he names are jealousy, envy, avarice, revenge, suspicion, deceit, slyness, guilt, vanity, conceit, ambition, pride and humility. Darwin points out that 'it is doubtful whether the greater number of the above

65

complex states of mind are revealed by any fixed expression, sufficiently distinct to be described or delineated' (p. 261). He gives the example of art. Painters cannot portray directly a person in the grip of a complex emotion, rather the painting has to include other persons or objects, 'accessories which tell the tale' (p. 79). However, if a complex emotion erupts into impassioned physical action, the clear, recognizable behavior pattern of an innate emotion takes its place. For example, guilt is ordinarily indistinct, subtle and difficult to detect. But when it shows, it seems to take on many of the expressive qualities of shame, that is, squirming, hiding, eyes averted, head hanging down. Regarding certain other complex emotions, Darwin observes:

> A man may have his mind filled with the blackest hatred or suspicion, or be corroded with envy or jealousy, but as these feelings do not at once lead to action, and as they commonly last for some time, they are not shown by any outward sign, excepting that a man in this state assuredly does not appear cheerful or good-tempered. If indeed these feelings break out into overt acts, rage takes their place, and will be plainly exhibited.
>
> (Darwin 1872, p. 79)

Darwin seems to suggest that the complex emotions, hatred, suspicion, envy and jealousy have at their core a single innate affect, that is, Rage. But I wonder whether the complex emotions may involve more than one innate affect. His use of the word 'complex' suggests a complicated structure made up of different interconnected parts. If jealousy erupts, it becomes Rage, but there may also be fluctuations of Shame and Grief. Hatred seems to exhibit the expressive actions of Contempt as well as Rage. Stewart suggests that the complex emotions are mixtures and modulations of the innate emotions that develop in the family. We will explore this question in the next chapter, and again in the discussion of movement themes that come from the shadow, the personal unconscious.

To summarize so far, Darwin was the first to differentiate between the fundamental emotions that are innate and the complex emotions that seem to derive from the innate affects. The expressive behavior of an innate emotion is easy to recognize. By contrast, the expressive behavior of a complex emotion tends to be subtle, indistinct, idiosyncratic. In addition to his wide-ranging study of the innate emotions, and a brilliant but too brief observation and discussion of the complex emotions, Darwin hints at a third category of emotional expression. He gives the example of certain gestures that one might think are innate because they're so familiar and easy to 'read.' But they're not innate and they're not universal. They seem to be limited to a particular culture (pp. 218–19). As we continue to discuss the nature of the individual affects, it will be helpful to differentiate between the innate emotions, the complex emotions and the symbolic cultural gestures. It may also be helpful to remember that every innate emotion has many names that express its wide range of intensity, from mild to extreme. With these thoughts in mind we are led to contemporary studies of the individual affects.

After Darwin the contribution of Silvan S. Tomkins (1962, 1963, 1982) has had the greatest influence on contemporary studies of the individual affects. His two-volume work entitled *Affect, Imagery, Consciousness* (1962, 1963) played a pivotal role in the current renewal of interest in the affects (Ekman 1972, 1989; Eibl-Eibesfeldt 1972; Izard 1977; Stewart and Stewart 1979; Stewart 1985, 1987a; Nathanson 1987).

Tomkins' interest in the affects began in the early 1940s when American psychology was still in the thrall of behaviorism. At that time studies of the affects, consciousness and the unconscious were considered unreliable and disreputable. Even so, Tomkins sensed intuitively that affect is important and designed a picture arrangement test that measures affect (pictures of happy, sad or angry faces) as one of the central variables. But he could offer no theoretical rationale for what he had done.

His early interest in computer simulation led him to conceptualize about the affects as amplifiers of other psychic functions. Then in the midst of such abstract thoughts, a real human baby came into his life. His first son was born in 1955 during a sabbatical year:

I observed him daily, for hours on end. I was struck with the massiveness of the crying response. It included not only very loud vocalization and facial muscular responses, but also large changes in blood flow to the face and engagement of all the striate musculature of the body. It was a massive, total-body response, which, however, seemed to center on the face. Freud had suggested that the birth cry was the prototype of anxiety, but my son didn't seem anxious. What, then, was this facial response? I labeled it *distress*. In the following months, I observed intense excitement on his face as he labored to shape his mouth to try to imitate the speech he heard. He would struggle minutes on end and then give up, apparently exhausted and discouraged. I noted the intensity of his smiling response to his mother and to me, and again I became aware that nothing in psychoanalytic theory (or any other personality theory at this time) paid any attention to the specificity of enjoyment as contrasted with excitement.

(Tomkins 1982, p. 354)

From the experience of watching his infant son, Tomkins recognized and identified the single major affect which Darwin had overlooked, that is Interest, with its range of intensity from interest to excitement. When considering the reason for the oversight, Tomkins wonders whether Darwin might have confused the sustained quality of the affect Interest with the thinking function. Tomkins holds that Interest is activated by or accompanies the drives, as well as certain reflexes and functions. Interest-Excitement is an intrinsic, energic aspect of sexuality, hunger, orientation reactions, reverie and reflective problem-solving as well as looking at or listening to something 'interesting' (Tomkins 1962, p. 339).

In Tomkins' view, the affects are the primary, innate, biological motivational system of the higher mammals, including human beings. The drives and other responses are secondary. The drives are secondary because they require amplification from the affects in order to function. For example, in a state of depression, the affect Interest is withdrawn from life's activities. Without Interest to amplify the hunger drive, we lose our appetite for food. Thus the hunger drive or the sexual drive or any other drive must be amplified by the appropriate affect if it is to work at all. Affect not only amplifies the drives, but it serves to motivate memory, perception, thought and action as well.

Tomkins differentiates three categories of affect that have developed in the evolutionary process: the 'positive' affects (which we seek to maximize), the 'negative' affects (which we seek to minimize) and a 'resetting' affect. He distinguishes eight innate affects. The 'positive' affects are Interest and Joy. The 'negative' affects are Distress, Fear, Anger, Contempt and Shame. The 'resetting' affect is Surprise (1962, 1963). The function of the 'positive' affects is to enable humans and the higher mammals to be excited by novelty (Interest); and to enjoy communion with and relationship to the familiar, especially those we love (Joy). The function of the 'negative' affects is to deal with the inevitable life crises that occur. Each of the 'negative' affects (Distress, Fear, Anger, Contempt, Shame) are adaptive not only to survival of the species, but to the development of individual values and consciousness as well. The function of the 'resetting' affect (Surprise) is that it interrupts all of the other affects, to enable instant reorientation whenever necessary.

For Tomkins the affects have evolved as a more flexible system to support increasingly complex forms of life. In a stable environment, the most simple life forms survive well on programmed instinct. But when we have to cope with a changing environment, survival depends on whether we can respond in flexible ways. To use the analogy of an evolutionary ladder, wherever the drive system is autonomous, we leave the complexity of the higher mammals and descend to the level of programmed instinct. Wherever the affect system is developed, we leave those basic organisms and ascend toward the most complex forms of life (Tomkins 1962, p. 150).

Based on his view of affect as prime motivating force, Tomkins calls for a complete revision of classic psychoanalytic theory regarding the primacy of the drives. Major errors come from the confusion of drive and affect. In speaking of Freud, Tomkins (1962) writes:

> Had he been able to continue his early posture – that mental disease is a disorder of the feelings – his system would not have been forced into that kind of reductionism which issued in the doctrine of sublimation, in the doctrine that aggression is a drive and finally in the doctrine of the death instinct. He could have had and eaten his biological cake had he not insisted on equating biological motives exclusively with the drives.
>
> (ibid., p. 127)

Tomkins' study is beautifully written, comprehensive and thoroughly documented. In addition to the material outlined above, he explores the innate neural programs that activate each of the primary affects, with particular attention to changes in density and level of neural stimulation. His contribution includes animal studies, a discussion of 'backed up affect' and a brief affective biography of Freud. He offers a great deal of information and

69

thought that is of importance to our topic. I recommend his work to the interested reader (1962, 1963, 1982).

Following Tomkins, Ekman (1972) and Izard (1977) are two leading contemporary investigators in the field of human emotion. Ekman and his colleagues and associates focus on the complexity of the face, particularly measurement of facial action. Izard's studies include the face, but he gives more attention to the role each of the primary emotions play in the development of consciousness, cognition and action. Both men were influenced by Tomkins who served as advisor to their early cross-cultural studies. These and subsequent studies have fully confirmed Darwin's views on the innate emotions and their universal forms of expression.

Chapter Nine

STEWART'S AFFECT AND ARCHETYPE

As we consider the bridge between contemporary affect studies and the psychology of C.G. Jung, we are led to Louis H. Stewart's 'Affect and archetype: A contribution to a comprehensive theory of the structure of the psyche' (1985). He proposes a new hypothesis as to the nature of the affects, individually and as a system, and the relation of the affects to other functions of the psyche.

Stewart was led to psychology through his experiences as an art student and then as a nursery and kindergarten teacher in a program that was based on the arts. His work with young children led him to see that development and creativity are basically the same process.

> I could see that the children were passing through stages of an autonomous process of creative development that found expression in their painting, dancing, singing, dramatics and play. The process followed orderly, regulated stages of exploration and assimilation, which led to imaginative play and creative work, and to a centering process that found expression in typical mandala paintings. I saw similar forms in their play and other creative activities.
>
> This was a revelation. I suddenly saw that the development of the whole individual was the same process as the process we call creativity, which we envy and honor so much in the creative artist, poet, religious innovator, philosopher, and social reformer. When years later I had become immersed in Jung's analytical psychology, and experienced his ideas embodied in my own analysis and in my analytic work with others, it was always self-evident to me that what he described as the individuation process, which rests upon active imagination, was

71

precisely what I had observed years before in the kindergarten children. In that context we called it 'development.'

(Stewart 1986, p. 184)

Stewart became a Jungian analyst, a university professor, and he conducted research in child and family development. Analytic practice, teaching and research kept him involved with play, dreams, fantasy and active imagination. His studies of sandplay as active imagination (1977, 1978, 1981a, 1981b, 1982) led him to see that play and imagination are completely intertwined with the affects.

Building on the contributions of Jung, Henderson, Darwin and Tomkins, we will approach Stewart's hypothesis through the following topics:

1 Play and Imagination
2 The Archetypal Affects
3 The Complex Emotions
4 Imagination and Curiosity: Twin Streams of Libido
5 The Primal Self
6 The Realized Self

PLAY AND IMAGINATION

Children develop a sense of who they are through symbolic play. As adults we do the same thing, but call it active or creative imagination. The symbolic play of childhood is the embodiment of the imagination – and imagination is play, that is play with images. Play and imagination function as the dynamic source of mythic consciousness.

Stewart's first study of the relationship of the affects to play and imagination was written in collaboration with his brother Charles Stewart who is a pediatrician and child psychiatrist. Stewart and Stewart (1979) explore the specific ways that play and imagination are interwoven with the affects.

First, play is the prototypical response to the affect of Joy. Joy motivates play. This leads to the recognition that affect (Joy) provides the energy that motivates play.

Next, the symbolic play of childhood leads children to recapitulate the emotionally charged experiences in their lives. Symbolic play involves spontaneous re-enactment of difficult situations that the child has been through. But play is completely voluntary. And no matter how difficult the content, it is fun. Here the child gets to control the situation; roles are often reversed. The process of symbolic play takes the child directly to and through the emotional core of the upsetting experience. Through playful re-enactment and further imaginative development, the overwhelm-ing effects of the crisis emotions are modulated and transformed.

Examples of this kind of transformation come to mind from children's dance classes. The following stories were made up by the children themselves only moments before dance improvis-ation. The children are classmates in a creative ballet class, a lovely, imaginative group of 8–10-year-old girls:

Gail dances 'a puddle of mud.'
Yolanda and Donna dance 'two magic elves.'
The elves see the puddle of mud and feel sorry for it. They turn the mud puddle into a beautiful ballerina – but as she dances, they get jealous and worried that no one will pay any more attention to them – so they turn her into a star and she dances from far away in the sky.

Lucia dances 'a black bear who used to be a child.'
Norma dances 'the bear/child's younger (human) sister.'
The sister was out gathering flowers when she got frightened by the bear and ran away, dropping the bouquet. The bear picked it up, and suddenly remembered that she too, used to be a child who picked flowers. Remembering this broke the spell and the children rejoiced as they met again.

Karen dances a 'Plant.'
Fern dances a 'Bad Witch.'
Linda dances a 'Good Witch.'
Good Witch helps Plant to grow. Bad Witch pushes it down with her magic. Back and forth – it grows and withers. Then the Bad Witch turns Good Witch into a frog – but the Good Witch's magic is strong and she returns to her own form. Then she turns the Bad Witch into a Good Witch, and together they help the Plant grow.

(Chodorow n.d.)

The dance/dramas described above are particularly cohesive and satisfying. The first two dances seem to reflect the ongoing process of attempting to resolve feelings of rivalry, typically between older and younger siblings. The third seems to show the essential problem of living with a mother who is sometimes good and sometimes bad. Such dynamics do not reflect pathology but are basic to the nature of the family. In each dance an emotionally difficult situation is expressed, the problems are met and there is the experience of resolution and transformation.

But not all dance/dramas have a happy ending. Sometimes the emotional tone remains relatively untransformed:

Norma dances 'a toymaker.'
Marcia dances 'a Swiss doll.'
Irma dances 'a Japanese doll.'
Toymaker tries to finish putting on an arm or finishing bits of each doll. But each time he turns his back on one of them, it changes position. Then he winds them up too tight and they break.

Donna dances 'The King.'
Barbara dances 'The Fairy.'
Ursula and Diana dance 'Two Dancers.'
The King wanted to dance, but was jealous. The Fairy danced for him and was laughed at. Then the Fairy brought two dancers and they danced for everyone. The King became angry, then jealous. Finally he got tired and sad.

Anna dances 'a little girl.'
Sandra dances 'a Teddy Bear.'
Barbara dances 'a China doll.'
Beth dances 'a Jack-in-the-Box.'
The little girl puts her toys away and moonlight streams in making the toys dance. China Doll was told by the Moon Fairy not to dance, but the other toys urged her to and then Jack-in-the-Box jumped out at her and she broke.

(Chodorow n.d.)

These dance/dramas all have sad endings that leave a catch in the throat. My memory of the broken dolls is vivid, even so many years later. The children expressed difficult situations that could not be resolved that day. In the weeks and months to come, the spontaneous, imaginative process continued to develop, as they would often make up stories and improvise variations and different solutions around the same theme. Sometimes the symbolic situation continued to have a tragic ending, other times, there was a happy resolution. But either way, the children were deeply

74

involved, they loved doing it, and the dances they created were passionate and beautiful.

Stewart's work calls for a deeper understanding of the psychological function of play and the imagination. Just as imaginative play is essential to the development of every child, active imagination is essential to the individuation process of adults:

> Careful observation of the day to day experiences of children reveals that they are forever playing out whatever it is in their life that arouses emotion. But in their play, the effects of these emotions are transmuted through compensatory fantasies, liquidating or cathartic experiences, and the like. Thus one must conclude that during the period of development, play and fantasy serve a *transformative* function in the equilibration of the personality, and this makes it readily apparent why in analysis, active imagination serves an identical transformative function in the 're-creation' of the wholeness of personality.
>
> (Stewart 1987b, p. 133)

Before closing this part of our discussion, I will attempt to re-state how the affects are intertwined with play and the imagination. First, we remember that Joy *motivates* play. Second, we have seen that play has a *transformative* function; the crisis emotions are transformed in the process of play. To summarize these two important points: 1) affect *energizes* play. And 2) play *transforms* affect. These observations are related to the most basic functions of the psyche: 'The ... ways in which the affects are enmeshed with play and the imagination exemplify two fundamental and reciprocal aspects of the psyche, namely, *energy* and *transformation*' (Stewart 1987b, p. 133).

THE ARCHETYPAL AFFECTS

With the recognition that affect *motivates* play and that affect is *transformed* through play, Stewart's hypothesis began to take form. As he reflected on *affect as psychic energy*, he was led to questions about the nature of the libido. As he thought about the *transformation of affect*, he was led to questions about the transformative function of the Self.

Was it possible, for example, that such functions as the self, the symbolic cultural attitudes, and the ego functions could be related to specific affect energizers, and could libido, the life instinct, with its twin aspects of Eros and Logos be similarly energized? These were heady thoughts, yet they seemed inescapable once the example of play had become clear.

(Stewart 1985, p. 94)

The complexity of these questions led to a thorough review of theories of the affects. The most comprehensive work found was that of Silvan S. Tomkins (1962, 1963). The work of Tomkins reaches back to Darwin; it has stimulated recent affect studies and promises to influence future research as well (see above, pp. 67–70).

Tomkins' hypothesis supported Stewart's analysis of play, and supported his developing ideas about the energic and transformative role of affects in the psyche. However, Stewart points out that Jung had come to similar thoughts as early as 1907, 'namely that the affects are the primary motivating system of the psyche, and that they are the source of imagery and consciousness' (Stewart 1986, p. 189).

The part of Tomkins' theory that is new has to do with the identification of specific affects and their specific functions. Tomkins identifies a limited number of primary affects that are innate. He offers a carefully worked out hypothesis about how they evolved and the particular functions of each.

Tomkins' identification of three categories of affects was in accord with Stewart's developing hypothesis. The 'positive,' motivating, life enhancement affects (Joy and Interest) came to be understood by Stewart as the innate, energic source of libido, the life instinct. The crisis/survival affects that are transformed through play (Distress, Fear, Anger, Contempt, Shame) are understood as innate, protective response patterns of the primordial Self. The process of psychological development modulates and ultimately transforms the crisis/survival affects toward the development of imagery and new consciousness. Here we see the transformative function of the Self from its primal untransformed depths to the ultimate development of an individual.

Tomkins identifies only one affect in his third category: the 'resetting' affect is Surprise. Surprise, or the Startle response, interrupts all of the other affects to enable instant reorientation.

In adopting Tomkins' hypothesis, Stewart found that some slight modifications were necessary. In addition to approaching the affects from the perspective and with the terminology of depth psychology, Stewart proposes a different perspective on Contempt and Shame. In accord with the classic study by Helen Lynd

(1958) contempt and shame may be understood as two faces of a single bi-polar affect; its stimulus is rejection.

Whether one experiences Contempt or Shame is determined by the direction of Contempt toward oneself or toward the other. Consequently we speak of the archetypal affect Contempt/Shame.
(Stewart 1987b, p. 134)

In a recent report on his hypothesis, Stewart writes:

Briefly stated, the archetypal affects may be thought of as an innate, regulatory system of the psyche which functions as an unconscious energic, orientating and apperceptive/response system which has evolved to replace an earlier system of programmed instinct. It comprises a dynamic system of seven archetypal affects.
(Stewart,1987a, p. 40)

The seven innate archetypal affects are listed below; their ranges of intensity are shown in parentheses, and the life stimulus of each is shown in italic:

JOY
(Enjoyment–Ecstasy)   *Relationship to the Familiar*

INTEREST
(Interest–Excitement)   *Novelty*

SADNESS
(Distress–Anguish)   *Loss*

FEAR
(Apprehension–Terror)   *The Unknown*

ANGER
(Irritation–Rage)   *Restriction of Autonomy*

CONTEMPT/SHAME
(Dislike–Disgust/Embarrassment–
   Humiliation)   *Rejection*

STARTLE
(Surprise–Startle)   *The Unexpected*

Before we proceed further, it is important to remember that in addition to the seven innate affects, each with its own range of intensity, there are countless numbers of feelings and emotionally toned complexes. We shall now discuss these mixtures and modulations of the innate affects that are formed in the family crucible.

THE COMPLEX EMOTIONS

As far back as Darwin, differences have been observed between the innate affects with their universally recognized forms of expression and a second group of emotional states that seem to be understood as mixtures and developments of the innate affects (Darwin 1872, p. 261; Izard 1977, pp. 92–6; Ekman 1972, p. 19).

In Stewart's view, the limited number of innate archetypal affects are clearly distinguished from the myriad complex emotions. The complex emotions (or feelings, affective complexes) are mixtures, modulations and transmutations of the innate affects. In his discussion about the nature of the affective complexes, Stewart suggests that they develop in the family crucible. All of the innate affects

> inevitably become enmeshed in the web of interpersonal relationships, transformed and intermingled to create such subtle and complex emotions as jealousy, envy, greed, anxiety, depression, as well as respect, admiration, compassion, mercy, reverence and the like. But in contrast to the innate, primal affects, these are affective complexes, the emotions and feelings that develop in the family.
>
> (Stewart 1987b, p. 154)

IMAGINATION AND CURIOSITY: TWIN STREAMS OF LIBIDO

For Stewart, Joy and Interest are the energic, affective source of libido. He proposes that the dynamism of joy is play (imagination); the dynamism of interest is curiosity (exploration).

> In the course of this study it ... became apparent that the imagination has a twin which finds its expression in the affect of Interest and in the dynamism of 'curiosity.' Moreover one sees that play (i.e. imagination) and curiosity are inseparably entwined in a dialectical process in which each potentiates the other.
>
> (Stewart 1987b, p. 133)

Play and curiosity are the early developmental forms of Jung's two kinds of thinking: fantasy thinking and directed thinking (Jung 1912a; Stewart 1985). They are also related to the syzygy (anima and animus) and the cosmogonic principles of Eros and Logos.

The fate of the libido is the decisive issue in life and in the process of individuation. It makes all the difference in the world whether or not libido is freely available for the tasks of life and for the realization of the Self. Marriage and family and the future generations depend upon a zest for life fully realized in imaginative playfulness and divine curiosity.

(Stewart 1987d, p. 387)

Chapter Ten

THE PRIMAL SELF

To continue our discussion of Stewart's hypothesis, we shall approach the Self from two perspectives: the source (i.e. the primal Self) and the goal (i.e. the realized Self).

ORGANIZING PRINCIPLE OF THE PRIMAL SELF

In its innate form the primal Self remains the same in the mature adult as it is in the new-born infant. Similar perhaps to the structure of the DNA molecule, or Jung's analogy of the preformed lattice in a crystalline solution, the primal Self contains the invisible 'groundplan' or innate potential toward the development of the human personality. As we know, the development occurs through the interweaving of innate potential with environmental influence.

The primal Self seems to be organized as a quaternity structured around a center. The typical mandala symbol that has been found in every culture throughout human history is an expression of such a fourfold structure. The circle around a cross is one of the earliest God-images, a universal symbol that represents the union of opposites within a totality. In *Aion* (1951) Jung discusses the a priori (i.e. innate) presence of these symbols in the psyche:

> Although 'wholeness' seems at first sight to be nothing but an abstract idea ... it is nevertheless empirical in so far as it is anticipated by the psyche in the form of spontaneous or autonomous symbols. These are the quaternity or mandala symbols, which occur not only in the dreams of modern people who have never heard of them, but are widely disseminated in the historical records of many peoples and many epochs. Their significance as *symbols of unity and totality* is amply confirmed by history as well as by empirical psychology. What at first looks like an abstract

idea stands in reality for something that exists and can be experienced, that demonstrates its a priori presence spontaneously.

(Jung 1951, p. 31)

In discussing the fourfold phenomenology of the Self and its structure around a center, Stewart draws the analogy to the fourfold structure of the DNA molecule, with its four amino acid compounds, adenine, guanine, cytosine and thymine. The twofold structure of the libido with its intertwining dialectic of joy and interest, brings to mind the corresponding energic image of sugar, ribose, which holds the compounds in the form of twin spirals, that is, the double helix. Stewart quotes Elizabeth Osterman in her important work entitled: 'The tendency toward patterning and order in matter and in the psyche.'

It is now known that these four constitute an alphabet by means of which matter communicates with matter. In combination with the sugar, ribose, they make a long threadlike compound, deoxyribonucleic acid (DNA), which is present in the central portion, the nucleus, of every living cell – of amoeba, flower or man.

(Osterman 1965, p. 18)

ARCHETYPAL AFFECTS OF THE PRIMAL SELF

It is at this a priori level of the primal Self that Stewart proposes the origins of a system of seven archetypal affects: Joy, Interest, Sadness, Fear, Anger, Contempt/Shame, Startle. Their development is shaped through a two fold structure of psychic energy that intertwines the affects of the libido (Joy and Interest) in an ongoing dialectic. In addition there is the quaternary structure around a center that contains the four primal affects of existential crises (Sadness, Fear, Anger and Contempt/Shame). These are structured around a fifth primal affect that has a centering function (Startle).

They appear to have evolved as a kind of self protective system which sensitizes the psyche to the fundamental spiritual crises of life, namely: *loss of a loved one* (Sadness); *the unknown* (Fear); *threat to autonomy* (Anger); *rejection* (Contempt/ Shame); and *the unexpected* (Surprise).

(Stewart 1987d, p. 393)

81

The constellation of an archetypal affect occurs when an innate primal image is in some way mirrored by a corresponding life experience. It is as if the inner image and the outer experience are two parts of the same symbolic stimulus. When the two parts recognize each other, they unite to form the symbol that releases the emotion. One aspect of the symbol is conscious (the life experience); the other part remains unconscious (the innate image/ imprint). Ethologists seem to be describing a similar process when they speak of the 'innate releasing mechanism' [Tinbergen] or the 'key tumbler' structures that release patterns of instinctive behavior in animals and humans (Stevens 1983, pp. 56–8).

INNATE IMAGE IMPRINTS

Through his study of the archetypal affects and the life experiences that stimulate them, Stewart was faced with the question: What might be the unconscious aspect of the symbols that constellate the primal affects? What might be the innate images or imprints?

> The aspect of the symbol that is represented in consciousness is the 'stimulus', for example, 'the unknown' in the case of terror. What then is the aspect of the symbol which is unconscious? This we assume must be an innate, primal image/imprint, or the potential for such an image/imprint. And how do we determine what these innate potential images may be? Traditional sources are the images of myth and fairy tale, as well as cultural symbols, in religion particularly, and, of course, dreams and the experiences of analysis. The question then posed is what are the universal primal images? Once put this way the answer seemed self-evident. The innate image/imprints could be but the images of pre-creation, and the dawning of consciousness: the abyss of terror, the void of anguish, the chaos of rage, and the alienation of disgust/ humiliation. With this recognition came another. The archetypal affects are themselves these image/imprints, that is to say, the state of consciousness produced by the *abaissement du niveau mental* which characterizes a specific affect, *is* the experience of the unconscious image/imprint. This does not mean that it is the noumenal form of the image/imprint as an unconscious potential. That will always remain a mystery. What we experience is the typical, and also personal form that it acquires in the process of becoming conscious.
>
> (Stewart 1987a, p. 42)

The *abyss*, *the void*, *chaos* and *alienation* are prominent images in the world's creation myths (Campbell 1949, pp. 271–2; Eliade 1967, pp. 83–131; Schaya 1971, pp. 61–73 and pp. 101–15). The first three (the void, the abyss, chaos) tend to be used interchangeably to describe the pre-existing state out of which the world was created. The fourth image (alienation) is also present from the beginning. In Jewish tradition the state of *galut* or exile is caused by the *alienation* of Yahweh from his feminine aspect, the Shekhina (Gross 1983). As I understand the *Zohar*, the act of creation was a fully mutual, passionate embrace. As the receptive *void* was filled with divine luminosity, there are references to orgasmic contractions. Then the Shekhina descended (or her chariot was plunged) into the depths of the *abyss* where the earthly realm began to emerge out of *chaos*. Similar to other Earth Goddesses, the Shekhina permitted her own body to be used as the foundation of the universe. From then on, instead of attending to their relationship, Yahweh got involved with His Chosen People and seemed to forget that the Shekhina had ever existed. From time to time He remembers Her; the Song of Songs comes to mind. She also returns as Wisdom in the Book of Job. But as a whole, since the Creation, Yahweh has denied and rejected his feminine aspect.

In Genesis too, *alienation* is patterned into the creation. The experience of alienation occurs when Adam and Eve eat the fruit of the tree of knowledge of good and evil. As they experience the toxicity of Shame, they are banished from paradise.

Let us take a moment to reflect on these *images* that are at the same time *experiences* of the primal affects. To experience the reality of the *void* is the actual, empty feeling of Sadness; to be at the edge of the *abyss* or to fall into it is the actual, bottomless gasp of Fear; to experience *chaos* is the feeling of being tied up in knots, that is the terrible muddle and frustration of Anger; to experience *alienation* is the actual withering rejection we feel (toward the other, or toward one's self) in Contempt/Shame.

The following list is a review of the archetypal affects and two aspects of their symbolic stimuli. The affect is listed to the left. The innate image/imprint is shown in the middle column. The corresponding life experience that presents itself to consciousness is shown on the right in italics. Only the fourfold primal affects are listed. The innate image/imprints of the other archetypal affects are less well understood, so have not yet been presented.

SADNESS	The Void	*Loss*
FEAR	The Abyss	*The Unknown*
ANGER	Chaos	*Restriction*
CONTEMPT/SHAME	Alienation	*Rejection*

THE PRIMAL AFFECTS AND THE SENSES

Before closing our discussion of the primal Self, I want to look at Stewart's idea (1987c) that there is a link at the primordial level between the affects and the senses. As I understand this material, Stewart proposes a psychological relationship between the senses (touch, hearing, sight, smell, taste, kinesthetic) and the primal affects (Sadness, Fear, Anger, Contempt/Shame, Startle). He suggests that the senses and the primal affects amplify each other and that the senses may have been the early precursors of the primal affects. The senses may be organized psychologically as a fourfold structure (touch, hearing, sight, smell/taste) formed around a central sense that has to do with orientation (the proprioceptive or kinesthetic sense).

To illustrate:

Sadness is our response to the loss of a beloved person or object. The sense of *touch* is central to experiencing the full impact of loss; our constant longing is for the embodied presence of the one we miss.

Fear has to do with our response to the unknown. The sense of *hearing* seems to be a direct link to that intangible realm.

Anger has to do with protecting oneself against attack, or protecting oneself against anyone or anything that threatens our autonomy. The sense of *seeing* is central to our ability to identify the threat and protect ourselves against it.

Contempt/Shame has to to with an evaluative response that finds others or ourselves unacceptable, unworthy. Similar to the affect Contempt, the sense of *smell* evaluates the external 'other;' similar to the affect Shame, the sense of *taste* evaluates something within oneself, that is, something that is inside our mouth or stomach. Together, *smell/taste* forms a bi-polar sense that is presumably related on a primal level to the rejection of noxious substances, from without and within.

Startle is the affect of centering, orientation and re-orientation; it is our response to the unexpected. On the instinctive body level, the *kinesthetic and proprioceptive* senses keep us centered and oriented.

Plate 1 The joy of dance.

Plate 2 With kindergarten children: 'Finding a caterpillar ...'
© Chuck Newman.

Plate 3 ' ... and emerging as butterflies.'
© Chuck Newman.

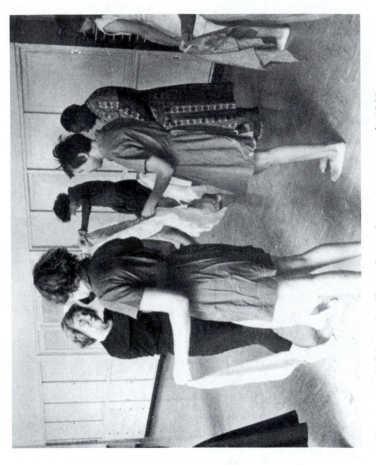

Plate 4 Trudi Schoop leading a dance therapy group, early 1960s.
© Ernest E. Reshovsky. Reproduced courtesy of Trudi Schoop.

Plate 5   Trudi Schoop teaching dance therapy, mid 1980s.
© Hugo Lörtscher, photographer of the Swiss School for Sports,
Magglingen, Switzerland. Reproduced courtesy of Ursula Weiss.

Plate 6 Trudi Schoop leading a training group for therapists, Switzerland, mid 1980s. © Hugo Lörtscher, photographer of the Swiss School for Sports, Magglingen, Switzerland. Reproduced courtesy of Ursula Weiss.

Plate 7 Trudi Schoop leading a training group for therapists, Switzerland, mid 1980s.
© Hugo Lörtscher, photographer of the Swiss School for Sports, Magglingen, Switzerland.
Reproduced courtesy of Ursula Weiss.

Plate 8   Mary Starks Whitehouse, 1978.
© Carolyn Caddes. Reproduced courtesy of Janet Adler.

Plates 9 and 10 Mary Whitehouse observing mover(s) in her studio, early 1960s.
© Irving Manning. Reproduced courtesy of Jane Manning.

The first four minutes of a much longer sequence of dance/movement as active imagination.

Plate 11 Mover closes her eyes and waits for an impulse to move her ...

Plate 12 as she allows the movement to unfold ...

Plate 13   ... a figure from a recent dream appears

Plate 14   they interact ...

Plate 15 and 16 'The symbols of the self arise in the depths of the body' – C.G. Jung.
© Pauline Van Pelt.

Chapter Eleven

THE REALIZED SELF

Building on Jung's theory that the affects are the source of energy, imagery, value and new consciousness, Stewart came to see how the higher functions of the ego and the Self are structured into the psyche; they have evolved and are developed from the primal affects.

THE EGO FUNCTIONS

The functions of the ego include sensation, intuition, thinking and feeling. These are apperceptive functions that help us deal with the world. Jung writes:

> These four functional types correspond to the obvious means by which consciousness obtains its orientation. *Sensation* (or sense perception) tells you that something exists; *thinking* tells you what it is; *feeling* tells you whether it is agreeable or not; and *intuition* tells you where it comes from and where it is going.
> (Jung 1961b, p. 219)

Sensation and intuition are implicative (i.e. immediate) modes of direct perception. Sensation senses the tangible; intuition senses the intangible. Thinking and feeling are explicative (i.e. rational or explainable) functions that deal with the fundamental ordering of experience. Thinking evaluates on a quantitative, logical, impersonal basis; feeling evaluates on a qualitative, organic, personal basis.

In Stewart's view Kant's *categories of understanding* (intellect) are the philosophical source of Jung's ego functions. Kant's implicative categories correspond to Sensation [objects in space] and Intuition [time and causality]; his explicative categories correspond to Thinking [quantitative logical order] and Feeling [qualitative organic order] (Stewart 1987b, p. 136 and p. 139).

THE FUNCTIONS OF THE CULTURAL SELF

The functions of the cultural Self include Henderson's four basic cultural attitudes: the aesthetic, the religious, the philosophic and the social – as well as a central, emerging, self-reflective psychological attitude. Each of the attitudes may be understood as a particular form of the imagination. And each offers a way to experience the life of the spirit.

The cultural attitudes are innate. For example, all children, if given the slightest opportunity, will express their fantasies through dance and song and paintings and drawings and clay and dramatic play (aesthetic imagination). Similarly, all children have fantasies about the Unknown, the world of angels, ghosts, spirits and things-that-go-bump-in-the-night – even infants have sleep rituals, wordless, self-comforting, repetitive actions, so similar to prayers, to ease the transition from the day world to sleep (religious imagination). Every child asks endless questions and wonders about and imagines possible answers, as he or she seeks a rational explanation of the order of the universe (philosophic imagination). And every child has to grapple with feelings about being included or excluded, and has fantasies about how to get along with others (social, ethical, moral imagination). A child's potential to develop all of the cultural forms is innate. The rest of the story has to do with genetic variations and the question of whether the child's environment will foster or inhibit cultural development in general and/or the development of a particular form. But the powerful emotions that are the source of artistic expression, religious ritual, philosophic/scientific inquiry and social relationships are innate.

Henderson (1984) characterizes the four main cultural attitudes: 'The ethical consistency of a social attitude, the logic of a philosophical attitude, the transcendent nature of a religious attitude ... the sensuous irrationality of the aesthetic attitude' (p. 49).

The aesthetic attitude seeks the world of beauty. * The relig-

* Naturally the world of beauty is not necessarily pretty. The great German artist, Kaethe Kollwitz writes of her work: 'My real motive for choosing my subjects almost exclusively from the life of the workers was that only such subjects gave me in a simple and unqualified way what I felt to be beautiful. For me the Koenigsberg longshoremen had beauty; the

ious attitude seeks the realm of the sacred. The philosophic attitude seeks principles of universal validity. The social attitude
seeks a state of communal well being, utopian communitas. As we
see, the cultural attitudes lead us to the age-old ideals of ultimate
human value: the Beautiful, the Holy, the True and the Good. The
functions of the cultural Self are mirrored in the external cultural
forms of Art, Religion, Philosophy and Society.

From the time of the ancient Greeks, the process of self-
knowledge has been recognized as one of the ultimate human
values. 'Know thyself' is an inscription at the Delphic Oracle. The
four cultural attitudes (aesthetic, religious, philosophic, social)
converge toward a fifth inner attitude that has to do with self-
knowledge, self-realization. Henderson speaks of a self-reflective
psychological attitude that functions as a kind of quintessence of
the other four. Through this central inner attitude, we develop
self-reflective consciousness.

As I understand Stewart, both the functions of the ego and the
functions of the cultural Self are structured in the psyche during
childhood through an interaction of the libido with the world and
the Self. The dynamism of Curiosity/Exploration is of particular
importance to the development of the ego functions. The dynamism of Play/Imagination is of particular importance to the development of the functions of the cultural Self. The ego functions
may be understood as innate, apperceptive *categories of the intellect*.
The functions of the cultural Self may be understood as innate,
expressive *categories of the imagination*.

In Stewart's view the primal affects and the differentiated functions are organized as quaternities structured around a center. At
the level of the primordial unconscious, we find the fourfold primal affects (Sadness, Fear, Anger, Contempt/ Shame) structured
around the affect of centering and orientation (Startle). At the
level of the cultural unconscious, we find the fundamental cultural
attitudes (aesthetic, religious, philosophic, social) structured
around a central, self-reflective psychological attitude. At the level
of the personal unconscious and ego consciousness, we find the
fourfold ego functions (sensation, intuition, thinking, feeling)
structured around a centering function that might best be
described as orientation.

Polish *jimkes* on their grain ships had beauty; the broad freedom of movement in the gestures of the common people had beauty' (1988, p. 43).

THE PRIMAL AFFECTS AND THE HIGHER FUNCTIONS

Each of the fourfold primal affects has two fundamental aspects: an apperceptive aspect and an expressive aspect. Stewart has suggested that the ego functions have presumably evolved from the apperceptive aspect; the cultural attitudes from the expressive aspect. The following pages will review the fourfold primal affects and the higher functions that appear to have evolved from them.

Sadness

When we experience *loss*, we may become identified with the *void*. Darwin describes a 51-year-old widow in an asylum who 'fancied that she had lost all her viscera, and that her whole body was empty' (Darwin 1872 p. 183). On an infant level it feels as if no one is out there. As adults, our longing for the lost loved one takes us into sobbing, weeping, lamentations and other rhythmic expressions of mourning. 'She wore an expression of great distress and beat her semi-closed hands rhythmically together for hours' (ibid.). It brings so much pain that we might ask: what is the use of Sadness? To approach an answer to this question, Stewart suggests that we let ourselves imagine what life might be like if there were no Sadness. If we didn't have to pay attention to loss, there would be little recognition of the significance to us of those we love. Imagine the bland, indifferent quality of life if our response to the death of a child, spouse or friend were something like: 'Oh well, I guess that's it. Here today, gone tomorrow.' Sadness connects us not only to those we love, but to every aspect of the tangible world. To lose a loved one is to lose the abundance and beauty of nature. The mythic image here is Demeter's barren wasteland.

Apperceptive

As we sense the importance of our relationship to the *tangible world*, the element earth, the ego function of *sensation*, is activated.

Expressive

As we experience the full impact of loss, the traditional, rhythmic, rocking expressions of mourning and the iconic focus serve to keep the image of the lost beloved person before our eyes; lamentations develop toward poetry, songs, dances, paintings and sculpture. The expressive behavior of sadness is *rhythmic harmony*; it is the essence of the *aesthetic attitude*.

Fear

When we experience the *unknown*, it may feel as if we have fallen into the *abyss*. As children we imagine ghostly phantoms in the shadows of a darkened room. We learn to comfort ourselves with the silent prayer of sleep rituals (Stewart and Stewart 1979, p. 47). As adults in the face of the unknown, we may feel as if we are on the edge of a precipice: our hair stands on end. We shiver as an uncanny feeling travels through the back of the knees, into the groins and up the spine. All of our attention is directed to an encounter with the dreaded unknown. On the most primitive level fear fosters survival, we faint (play dead) or flee. With the development of consciousness, we tend to be drawn into a desperate, yet ongoing and continuous relationship with the intangible unknown.

Apperceptive

As we sense the presence of myriad intangible, *unknown* possibilities, the ego function of *intuition* is activated.

Expressive

The primal expression is uncontrollable repetitive action. As we engage in *rituals* to ward off demons or appease the Gods, there is a development toward the *religious* attitude:

> At bottom, the phenomenology of Fear can be understood only as a response to the 'unknown,' which in its spiritual aspect is Otto's 'Wholly Other,' and the 'abyss' of hellish terror. This is the channel of analogy which has led to the Religious Cultural Attitude. In *The Idea of the Holy* (1923), Rudolph Otto has shown in a compelling *tour de force* how the most exalted of religious feelings have evolved from the primal experience of terror, 'demonic dread.'
>
> (Stewart 1987b, p. 140)

Anger

When we experience *restriction*, we may be thrown into a state of *chaos*. On an infant or child level, it's a frantic state: thrashing about, kicking, scratching, biting. As adults we are taken over by the most primitive approach to problem solving. All attention is focused on how to 'get rid of' the cause of our frustration. At this level, to solve the problem means that we try to kill it.

What is the use of Anger? On a jungle level it is a matter of survival, just as it may be any time one is threatened by attack. Whether animal or human, Darwin (1872) points out that Anger 'gives strength to the muscles and at the same time energy to the will' (p. 239).

Apperceptive

Anger lets us know that our world has been turned upside-down – something is terribly wrong – everything's in chaos. As we begin to identify the perceived threat to our autonomy, our attention is fiercely focused on how to remove the intrusion that is creating such upheaval. As we identify the problem and begin to develop *strategies* to put things in order again, we approach an early stage of the ego function of *thinking*.

> Is this not a first stage in thinking, that is the identification and engagement with a problem? What follows then in subsequent reflection may be improved strategies for solving the problem. As we know from bitter experience, an angry outburst is often followed by a long period of 'rehashing' the situation: I could have said that, or why didn't I do such and such, and so on. This is thinking, pragmatic attempts to set things aright in one's own mind at least; still under the sway of the emotion, to be sure, but thinking nevertheless.
>
> (Stewart 1987b, p. 141)

Expressive

The expressive behavior of Anger, that is, threat and attack, is the most primitive form of reason. With the development of consciousness, we learn to attack certain problems symbolically. Here we recognize the furrowed brow, clenched fist and fiercely focused attention of a concentrating philosopher:

> The philosopher William James saw philosophy as an unusually stubborn attempt to think clearly, which captures a commonly held slant on the nature of a philosopher as one who thinks more deeply and obstinately than other people. The greatest frustration for a philosopher is not to understand something.
>
> (Stewart 1987b, pp. 141–2)

Whether the forceful attack of the jungle, or the emphatic gestures that punctuate scholarly arguments, the expressive behavior of Anger is *reason*; it is central to the *philosophic* attitude.

Contempt/Shame

When we experience *rejection*, we may be thrown into a state of *alienation*. Contempt/Shame is one of the most toxic of the affects. Most children and adults can talk about feeling sad, or afraid, or mad, but feelings of Contempt or Shame are rarely named. It is as if the experience is too embarrassing to admit, perhaps even to ourselves.

What is the use of Contempt/Shame? The affect seems to have evolved from '... the primal affective reflex whose function was the rejection of noxious, potentially poisonous, substances. In the extremity of Disgust one may still experience this primal reaction of vomiting' (Stewart 1987b, p. 150). At the barnyard level the antecedent to the affect Contempt/Shame is expressed through a 'pecking order.' The dominance and submission behavior of many mammals is similarly related to establishment of a hierarchical social structure. Social customs differ from one culture to another, but all are concerned with status, deference and the mediation of human relationship.

Apperceptive

Stewart describes Contempt/Shame as

> an acute evaluative function which finds others or ourselves wanting. When we are contemptuous of others we turn up our noses and then find ourselves alienated; when we experience someone else's, or our own, contempt we hang our heads in shame, and find ourselves alienated. Nothing in the world has such a potential for inducing us to take stock of ourselves and our relationships with others.
>
> (1987b, p. 153)

As the affect forces us to grapple with the bitter experience of alienation, we develop *sensibilities* that help us evaluate the subtle and complex network of human relationships. This seems to be an early stage of the ego function of *feeling*.

Expressive

Contempt/Shame forces full attention on our place in the human community. This punishing affect is always expressed within the context of a *relationship* (either with one's self or with another); it is central to the evolution and development of the *social* attitude.

RHYTHM, RITUAL, REASON, RELATIONSHIP

Just as the dynamic expression of Joy is play, and the dynamic expression of Interest is curiosity, each of the crisis affects has its own expressive dynamism that has evolved with the human species. As described above, the expressive dynamism develops from a completely untransformed, primal state toward the higher functions of the ego and the Self. Stewart (1987b, pp. 138–43) suggests the terms Rhythm, Ritual, Reason and Relationship as a way to remember something of the essence of each of these expressive, transformative processes. As we have seen, Sadness is expressed and transformed through rhythm and rhythmic harmony. Fear is expressed and transformed through ritual. Anger is expressed and transformed through reason, primitive and differentiated. Contempt/Shame is expressed and transformed through relationship.

Another perspective on the affects and their expressive dynamisms can be seen in the universal games that have been played since antiquity in every part of the world. Stewart points out that 'the universal games constellate specific emotions or sets of emotions which are equilibrated in the process of playing the games' (1987a, p. 37). The structure of the commonly played games consistently demonstrate a four-fold categorization (Caillois 1958; Roberts and Sutton-Smith 1970; Stewart and Stewart 1979; Stewart 1987a). In the appendix we shall take a brief look at the following categories: games of *physical skill*, games of *chance*, games of *strategy* and *central person* games.

THE COMPENSATORY IMAGES

Jung describes the psyche as a *complexio oppositorum*, a complex of opposites. Any one-sided position will automatically be compensated by the constellation of its opposite. The constellation of opposites may produce an inner condition of tension, conflict and discord that is uncomfortable. But there seems to be an important psychological purpose to it all, that is, it insures a development toward wholeness of personality. The process ultimately leads to the realization of the Self.

Each of the innate, primal image/imprints, the *void* of Sadness, the *abyss* of Terror, the *chaos* of Rage and the *alienation* of Contempt/Shame, has a compensatory image/imprint. The emptiness of the *void* is compensated by the abundant *beauty of nature*. The *abyss* is compensated by the *holy mountain*. *Chaos* is compensated by the *ordered cosmos*. *Alienation* is compensated by *utopian communitas*. As we look at them, we find pairs of images that span the heights and depths of human emotional experience. Reflecting the compensatory nature of the psyche, when one image is in consciousness, its opposite is to be found in the unconscious.

> If the ... archetypal affects have necessarily evolved as an affective system of apperception and response, a kind of psychological immune system to protect the self, so to speak, which reacts autonomously to the archetypal crises of life, then we must also assume that this has required the evolution of potential image/imprints appropriate to the life of humans, which includes a spiritual dimension. Clearly the images we have introduced ... are indicative of the highest of human values; in fact they are immediately recognizable as the age old categories of the holy, the beautiful, the true and the good, which have everywhere found expression in the cultural forms of religion, art, philosophy and society.
>
> These categories, which are representative of the cultural attitudes, the religious, the aesthetic, the philosophical and the social, may perhaps be thought of in their totality as a form of the 'ultimate self' (Henderson 1984). . . . That is to say, they have phylogenetically evolved, and are ontogenetically developed, out of the archetypal affects of the primal self.
>
> (Stewart 1987a, p. 43)

Here we see a fully embodied, integrated sense of the Self as it evolves out of the primordial depths toward the highest aspirations of the human spirit. To provide an overview of the various elements, I have adapted a table from Stewart's 'Affect and archetype in analysis' (1987b, p. 142). It reads from left to right, that is, from symbol and primal affect, to the evolved, differentiated functions (see figure 1).

Stewart's theoretical synthesis is original, provocative, stimulating, and deeply grounded in the experience of the body. He is the first to bring together Jungian thought and contemporary affect theory. His comprehensive view of the emotions and his conclusions provide a valuable clarification and systematization of the structure of the psyche, the dynamics of the psyche and psychological/symbolic development. These powerful images and experiences will be taken up again in the final section of the book as they are intrinsic to my discussion of clinical practice.

Figure 1 Stewart's Theoretical Synthesis

| | The Archetypal Affects of the Self | | Evolved, Differentiated Functions | |
| | Symbol and Primal Affect | | | |
Stimulus	Image	Affect	Expressive Dynamism / Noetic Apperception	Cultural Attitude / Ego Function
The Unknown	the Abyss	FEAR	Ritual / the Intangible	Religious Attitude / Intuitive Function
Loss	the Void	GRIEF	Rhythm / the Tangible	Aesthetic Attitude / Sensation Function
Restriction	Chaos	ANGER	Reason / Quantitative Order	Philosophic Attitude / Thinking Function
Rejection	Alienation	CONTEMPT/SHAME	Relationship / Qualitative Order	Social Attitude / Feeling Function
Unexpected	Disorientation	STARTLE	Reflection / Orientation	Psychological Attitude / Ego Consciousness
The Familiar	Illumination	JOY	Play / Being	Imagination / Eros (Relatedness)
The Novel	Insight	INTEREST	Curiosity / Becoming	Exploration / Logos (Discrimination)

Source: Stewart 1987b, p. 142

Chapter Twelve

CHILD DEVELOPMENT

A number of developmental theories have made a contribution to depth psychology. The ones most relevant to this work are grounded in normal development. I shall discuss a theory proposed by Stewart and Stewart (1979, 1981) that seeks to integrate aspects of the work of Piaget, Jung, Neumann, Erikson, and Sutton-Smith. I intend to concentrate on the critical first two years of the child's development with particular attention to the stages leading up to the discovery of 'pretend' and symbolic play.

Development occurs through the interaction of the child with the environment. The child's innate potential and environmental influences are usually of equal importance. An innate groundplan laid down in the DNA directs the infant's development in observable stages of increasing mobility, consciousness, and imaginative and intellectual understanding of the world and the self. The unfolding of this normal developmental plan can be encouraged or discouraged. Appropriate mirroring of the innate groundplan by the mother, father, culture and society is important.

Ordinarily, 'good enough' parenting means that there is a primary person (usually the mother) who is present and attentive to the child's basic needs for nurturing, comfort and loving playfulness. The essential qualities of Winnicott's 'good enough' mother have to do with her capacity for spontaneous play and natural curiosity. Stewart (1987a) expresses this simply and beautifully: 'Blessed indeed is the child who has a playful and curious mother!' (p. 38).

The process of individuation, that is to say, becoming a unique individual human being, is energized by the innate archetypal affects of Joy and Interest with their activated dynamisms of play and curiosity. Joy (play) and Interest (curiosity) engage in an ongoing dialectical relationship. Each potentiates the other. In their fully differentiated form Joy/Play and Interest/Curiosity may be understood as Eros, divine relatedness; and Logos, divine curiosity (see p. 78–9).

Thus as we shall see, each new stage of the infant's development represents an integration of a new level of mobility; a new level of consciousness; a new development in play/imagination, i.e. a new 'game'; and a new development in curiosity/exploration, i.e. a new 'interest.' In total each new stage may be described as the achievement of a new stage in the development of ego-Self identity. This is what Neumann refers to as the ego-Self axis. The experiential core of each passage in the development of identity is a startling, numinous moment of synthesis and reorientation.

I shall review five critical stages in normal development beginning with the first integration following birth and ending with the conscious awareness of the ability to 'pretend,' which occurs around 16 to 18 months of age. Conscious awareness of 'pretend' leads to the development of symbolic play and imagination. These stages may be labelled: 1) Uroboric wholeness; 2) the smile of recognition of the other; 3) the laughter of self-recognition; 4) object constancy; and 5) the awareness of pretend.

UROBORIC: UNION WITH THE SELF

The uroboros is a mythical image of a circular snake with its tail in its mouth. It is a characteristic symbol of the remote past, a state of wholeness, utter containment. Neumann relates it to 'the Great Round, in whose womb the ego-germ lies sheltered' (1973, p. 10). It is the experience of at once holding and being held. Shared rhythms of holding, touching, gazing, lulling and lullabies are the psychic nourishment of this earliest phase. Parent(s) and infant immerse in these together. The infant also does them when alone.

The first primal recognition of self may well be that powerful and comforting moment when thumb and mouth find each other.

We may see that the infant, while sucking its fingers or its toes, incarnates the image of the mythical Uroboros that, according to Neumann, represents the 'wholeness' of that undifferentiated state of self-other consciousness that is characteristic of this developmental state. We can also see in this early behavior the earliest evidence of that aspect of the autonomous process of individuation that Neumann, following Jung, has called *centroversion*. In this light we may understand the infant's behavior in the discovery of sucking its thumb as representing the first synthesis of the psyche following upon the rude disruption of life within the womb, which had more impressively represented a paradisiacal absorption in the purely unconscious process of life itself.

(Stewart 1986, p. 191)

The natural process of bringing thumb and mouth together is increasingly recognized as an important early developmental event. Greenspan and Greenspan refer to 'the challenge of finding your mouth – the reward of nature's pacifier' (1985, p. 31). The earliest meetings of mouth and thumb are usually transitory – before the mouth can really get hold of it, the thumb tends to wander away. But sooner or later, the hand reaches for the mouth and the thumb or fingers are surrounded and held. Not only the mouth, but the thumb too experiences the pleasurable, self calming sensations of rhythmic sucking. In this way we first learn that we are able to hold and comfort ourselves.

FIRST SMILE: RECOGNITION OF THE OTHER

Any fully spontaneous smile at any time in life has at its core the infant's smile, when she or he first consciously recognizes the now familiar sounds and face of the mother. When Joy and Interest come together, we begin to fall in love. Stewart (1984) reflects on the infant's first smile:

What are the first signs of love in the infant and child? Our Western image of childbirth has been that the mother must suffer and the child come crying into the world. All this has more recently been questioned and there are those who talk about infants entering the world with smiles on their faces and wide awake mothers ready to smile back immediately upon birth. We are far from knowing then what may be the possible potential of the development of love in the child. However, what is observable today is that the mutual smile of recognition between mother and infant does not occur for several weeks after birth. Before that the child smiles under certain conditions of satiety, half awake, half asleep, but in a dazed, glassy-eyed manner. Then there comes a moment, as early as the end of the first month sometimes, when the infant, awake and clear eyed, smiles in what is unmistakably a pleased recognition of the familiar sounds and face of the mother. Soon, within days or weeks, the infant's first joyful laugh occurs.

(ibid., p. 1)

FIRST LAUGH: RECOGNITION OF SELF

As the smile is a recognition of the Other, the laugh is a recognition of the Self. The infant's first spontaneous laughter when alone expresses joy in the sheer exuberance of bodily motion. This kind of laughter usually comes in the midst of self-movement, for example the kind of rhythmic leg kicking that reverberates through the infant's whole body until the entire world seems to join in. Or, the baby throws his or her head back and discovers that s/he is both the mover and the one who is moved. Piaget describes such a laugh:

It will be remembered that Laurent at 0;2(21) [2 months, 21 days], adopted the habit of throwing his head back to look at familiar things from this new position. At 0;2(23 or 24) he seemed to repeat this movement with ever increasing enjoyment and ever decreasing interest in the external result: he brought his head back to the upright position and then threw it back again time after time, laughing loudly.

(Piaget 1962, p. 91)

Natural laughter has at its core 'the spontaneous expression of the pure joy of being alive and ... is ... the prototype of play' (Stewart 1985, p. 93). From this point on, laughter will mark every new recognition of the self.

OBJECT CONSTANCY

Separation anxiety develops in the third quarter of the baby's first year. At the same time that the infant begins to struggle with the pain of separating from beloved persons, s/he immerses herself or himself in games of peek-a-boo, and intensely investigates problems of disappearance and re-appearance.

At 0;8(14): Jacqueline is lying on my bed beside me. I cover my head and cry 'coucou'; I emerge and do it again. She bursts into peals of laughter, then pulls the covers away to find me again. Attitude of expectation and lively interest.

(Piaget 1952, p. 50)

0;9(15): Jacqueline wails or cries when she sees the person seated next to her get up or move away a little (giving the impression of leaving).

(Piaget 1952, p. 249)

0;9(20): Jacqueline is lying down and holds her quilt with both hands. She raises it, brings it before her face, looks under it, then ends by raising and lowering it alternately while looking over the top of it: Thus she studies the transformation of the image of the room as a function of the screen formed by the quilt.

(Piaget 1954, p. 193)

As the first smile is the beginning of mother-child recognition, peek-a-boo and later games of hide-go-seek continue an ongoing process that leads to the development of object constancy.

AWARENESS OF PRETEND

Jung describes this major passage of consciousness as

the first morning of the world, the first sunrise after the primal darkness, when that inchoately conscious complex, the ego, the son of the darkness, knowingly sundered subject and object, and thus precipitated the world and itself into definite existence .... Genesis 1: 1–7 is a projection of this process.

(1963, par. 129)

A number of passages in the infant's first year create the base upon which a clear separation of day-world and dream-world can occur. Neumann (1954, 1973) refers to this differentiation of conscious and unconscious as 'separation of the world parents.' In the infant's life, this passage comes not through the word but rather through the discovery of nonverbal, symbolic play. The baby discovers that s/he can pretend.

Around sixteen to eighteen months of age, the child becomes aware of the semiotic function through the experience of pretense; for example in the miming of an already adaptive behavior pattern like the ritual behavior adopted to ease the transition into sleep (e.g., thumb sucking and fingering the satiny edge of a blanket). The child laughs with joy at this new recognition of Self; and this is pretend play (Piaget 1962). But let us reflect for a moment on the sleep ritual. This is not a neutral pattern of behavior. It represents one of the landmarks in the child's development. If the transition to sleep and waking is not easily accomplished, the child may be forever prone to sleep disturbances, to excessive fear of the dark, needing a night light, etc. And why is going to sleep difficult? Because it brings together the child's most feared and distressing fantasies, that of being deprived of the presence and comfort of those most dear, and of being left alone in the dark which is peopled by who knows what ghostly phantoms. Thus we consider it no accident that the child discovers pretense in the recognition of the sleep ritual; pretend play begins with the miming of a behavior pattern which has assisted the child in warding off fear of the unknown and soothing the anguish of separation. Subsequent pretend play will be seen to reenact all of the emotionally charged experiences of the child's life.

(Stewart and Stewart 1979, p. 47)

After the child recognizes his or her own sleep ritual, s/he teaches it to the dolls and stuffed animals. With the discovery of pretend, the child begins to play out an unending stream of imaginative enactments and intense little dramas. Imagination now becomes conscious and clearly visible through physical action. This first discovery of pretend coincides with the beginning of real curiosity about language. With this passage, the child enters the symbolic world.

Each of the stages we have discussed is associated with a particular quality of movement that is expressed alone and in relationship. In the final chapter on movement themes, I will describe five symbolic events that appear in dance movement. The symbolic actions and interactions correspond to the preverbal passages I have just presented. They are: 1) patterns of uroboric self-holding; 2) seeking the face of the witness and when found, a smile of recognition; 3) the laughter of self-recognition; 4) disappearance and reappearance; and 5) full engagement in the symbolic process via free, imaginative use of mime.

Chapter Thirteen

ACTIVE IMAGINATION

As we consider the link between depth psychology theory and practice, we are led to active imagination, Jung's analytical method of psychotherapy. I have mentioned it before, but shall take it up now in more detail.

After the break with Freud, Jung felt disoriented and sensed so much pressure inside himself that he suspected a psychic disturbance. Thinking there might be something in his past that was causing the pressure, he went over all the details of his entire life, twice, with particular attention to early memories. But he could find no logical explanation or solution.

Then he deliberately opened himself to the impulses and images of the unconscious and decided to do whatever occurred to him. The first thing that came up was a childhood memory. At the age of 10 or 11 there was a period when he was fascinated with building games. This memory of spontaneous play was accompanied by a rush of emotion. Jung, now in his middle years, felt out of touch with his own creative life. He realized that he had to re-establish a relationship to that inner child. But how was he to bridge the distance between himself, a grown man, and the young boy? Since there seemed to be no rational way to do it, he submitted to his fantasies and began to enact them, that is, play exactly as he had when he was a boy:

> As a grown man it seemed impossible to me that I should be able to bridge the distance from the present back to my eleventh year. Yet if I wanted to re-establish contact with that period, I had no choice but to return to it and take up once more that child's life with his childish games. This moment was a turning point in my fate, but I gave in only after endless resistances and with a sense of resignation. For it was a pain-

fully humiliating experience to realize that there was nothing
to be done except play childish games.

(Jung 1961a, p. 174)

We have to remember that the year was 1913. It was unheard
of for a bourgeois Swiss husband, father, doctor, university professor, to gather stones and sit by the side of the lake, building a
miniature village out of blocks, stones and mud! But despite feelings of humiliation, Jung remained engrossed with the task and
went on with the building game every day, weather permitting.

The small town he built included cottages, a castle, gates and
arches. Then he realized the church was missing and made a
square building with a dome. He knew the church needed an altar
too, but felt hesitant. It took him a long time to find the right
stone.

Suddenly I caught sight of a red stone, a four-sided pyramid
about an inch and a half high. It was a fragment of stone which
had been polished into this shape by the action of the water – a
pure product of chance. I knew at once that this was the altar.
I placed it in the middle under the dome, and as I did so, I
recalled the underground phallus of my childhood dream.

(Jung 1961a, p. 174)

As Jung placed the altar stone inside the church, a fearful
dream from early childhood came back to him. It had haunted him
for years but was then buried and forgotten. In the dream (1961a,
pp. 11–12) he descended into a large, subterranean temple where
he found a terrifying God of the Underworld. It was an enormous
ritual phallus set on a magnificent golden throne. Now, through
the process of symbolic play, he was led directly to the core of one
of his deepest complexes. He remembered this early dream again
and sought to understand its meaning.

Jung wrote his memoirs many years later when he was in his
eighties. By then, he understood that his childhood dream about
the fearful, underground God had a purpose:

Who spoke to me then? Who talked of problems far beyond my
knowledge? Who brought the Above and Below together, and
laid the foundation for everything that was to fill the second
half of my life with stormiest passion? Who but that alien guest
who came both from above and from below?

103

Through this childhood dream I was initiated into the secrets of the earth. What happened then was a kind of burial in the earth, and many years were to pass before I came out again. Today I know that it happened in order to bring the greatest possible amount of light into the darkness. It was an initiation into the realm of darkness. My intellectual life had its unconscious beginnings at that time.

(Jung 1961a, p. 15)

As Jung continued the process of imaginative play, his thoughts clarified. The pressure he had been feeling was released, as a flood of fantasies (that is, images and emotions) came to consciousness. He wrote them down as well as he could; he also drew and painted them. After giving the fantasies form, he made every effort to analyze and understand their meaning.

His building game turned out to be the beginning of a deep process of psychological development. In a beautifully written, thought provoking review of Jung's confrontation with the unconscious, Stewart (1982, p. 210) points out that play does not necessarily lead down the slope of memory to childishness; rather it leads directly to the unfinished business of childhood. Symbolic play inevitably involves some regression, because the process takes us to the emotional core of our complexes. But play does more. Symbolic play activates the image producing function of the psyche (i.e. the imagination) which puts us in touch with ourselves. In Jung's case, he not only retrieved long forgotten memories from his past; a flood of fantasies were released that ultimately reshaped his future.

The years when I was pursuing my inner images were the most important in my life – in them everything essential was decided. It all began then; the later details are only supplements and clarification of the material that burst forth from the unconscious, and at first swamped me. It was the *prima materia* for a lifetime's work.

(Jung 1961a, p. 199)

Jung came to call this process 'active imagination.' As a psychotherapeutic method, it has two parts. The first half is *letting the unconscious come up*. The second half consists in *coming to terms with the unconscious* (Jung 1973, p. 561). Another way of describing it is that you open to the unconscious and give free rein to fantasy; at the same time you maintain an alert, attentive, active point of view.

The starting point of active imagination is an emotional state that may take the form of a dream image, a fragment of fantasy, an inner voice, or simply a bad mood. Jung writes:

> To begin with, the task consists solely in observing objectively how a fragment of fantasy develops.
>
> (Jung 1929, p. 16)

> I ... took up a dream-image or an association of the patient's, and, with this as a point of departure, set him the task of elaborating or developing his theme by giving free rein to his fantasy. This according to individual taste and talent could be done in any number of ways, dramatic, dialectic, visual, acoustic, or in the form of dancing, painting, drawing, or modelling.
>
> (1947, p. 202)

> It is technically very simple to note down the 'other' voice in writing and to answer its statements from the standpoint of the ego. It is exactly as if a dialogue were taking place between two human beings with equal rights.
>
> (1916, pp. 88–9)

> He must make the emotional state the basis or starting point of the procedure. He must make himself as conscious as possible of the mood he is in, sinking himself in it without reserve and noting down on paper all the fantasies and other associations that come up. Fantasy must be allowed the freest possible play, yet not in such a manner that it leaves the orbit of its object, namely the affect .... The whole procedure is a kind of enrichment and clarification of the affect, whereby the affect and its contents are brought nearer to consciousness, becoming at the same time more impressive and more understandable.
>
> (1916, p. 82)

Quite often, the patients themselves feel that certain material contains a tendency to visibility. They say, for instance: 'That dream was so impressive, if I only could paint I would try to express its atmosphere.' Or they feel that a certain idea should be expressed not rationally but in symbols. Or they are gripped by an emotion which, if given form, would be explainable, and so on. And so they begin to draw, to paint, or to shape their images plastically, and women sometimes do weaving. I have even had one or two women who danced their unconscious figures. Of course, they can also be expressed in writing.

(1935, p. 173).

My most fundamental views and ideas derive from these experiences. First I made the observations and only then did I hammer out my views. And so it is with the hand that guides the crayon or brush, the foot that executes the dance-step, with the eye and the ear, with the word and the thought: a dark impulse is the ultimate arbiter of the pattern, an unconscious a priori precipitates itself into plastic form.

(1947, p. 204)

As the unconscious material was given form, Jung always sought to understand its meaning. He also drew ethical conclusions from it, to be put to work in life.

I took great care to try to understand every single image, every item of my psychic inventory, and to classify them scientifically – so far as this was possible – and, above all, to realize them in actual life. That is what we usually neglect to do. We allow the images to rise up, and maybe we wonder about them, but that is all. We do not take the trouble to understand them, let alone draw ethical conclusions from them. This stopping-short conjures up the negative effects of the unconscious.
    It is equally a grave mistake to think that it is enough to gain some understanding of the images and that knowledge can here make a halt. Insight into them must be converted into an ethical obligation. Not to do so is to fall prey to the power principle.

(Jung 1961a, pp. 192–3)

Some forms of active imagination are usually done by the patient alone, away from the analyst. Other forms such as sandplay and dance/movement usually include the presence of the analyst as witness. Early on in analysis, whether the endeavor is solitary or shared, the analytic relationship serves as container and process. But a long-term goal of active imagination is to liberate the patient through his or her own efforts rather than through dependence on the analyst. The analyst may serve as consultant and/or witness, but the process is self-directed and usually needs no interpretation. When Jung worked with patients who needed some kind of interpretive response, he made it as tentative as possible and returned their material to them through open-ended questions:

> I had to try to give provisional interpretations at least, so far as I was able, interspersing them with innumerable 'perhapses' and 'ifs' and 'buts' and never stepping beyond the bounds of the picture lying before me. I always took good care to let the interpretation of each image tail off into a question whose answer was left to the free fantasy activity of the patient.
>
> (Jung 1947, p. 203)

In his earlier works Jung speaks of active imagination and dream interpretation as two distinct psychotherapeutic methods. But if we follow the development of his thought, active imagination takes on an increasingly important role. In his later writings he says that his dream interpretation method is based on active imagination (Jung 1947, p. 205), and he describes active imagination as 'the analytical method of psychotherapy' (1975, p. 222). In his final work he relates active imagination to the entire alchemical process, the development of self-knowledge (Know Thyself) and the process of individuation (1963, pp. 494–9 and 526–31).

Eliade (1963) wrote: 'Life cannot be *repaired*, it can only be *recreated*' (p. 30). In analysis, active imagination is that re-creative process. Dance/movement is one of its forms.

Part Three

THE MOVING IMAGINATION

Chapter Fourteen

THE NATURE OF MY WORK

My work identity has changed many times: dance student, dancer, dance teacher, dance therapist, psychotherapist, psychoanalyst. The changes have not felt deliberate, rather they seemed to emerge out of an ongoing process. Being a dance student led to being a dancer. My need to stay connected to a certain creative source led me to teach children's dance. Work with children seemed to lead naturally to dance as therapy. Dance therapy led to psychotherapy and eventually to psychoanalysis. At each stage, I have been grateful for the resources of previous experience. Dance/movement has remained and continues to be an important part of my work.

I practice Jungian analysis in an office/studio that is at one end of my home. The room has a pair of comfortable chairs, a small table for beverages and some open space to move. One of the walls is covered with shelves holding hundreds of little sandplay figures waiting to enter the sandtray. There is an adjacent balcony area where I keep clay and other art materials.

Following Jung's late thought, I understand active imagination to be the fundamental method of analytic practice. The therapeutic relationship serves as container and process. Active imagination clearly includes the use of dance/movement, as well as sandplay and every kind of artistic media. But it also includes imaginative exploration of dreams, fantasies, memories, present life experiences and issues in the analytic relationship. From this larger perspective, work with the transference and countertransference can be a form of active imagination (Davidson 1966; Schwartz-Salant 1982; Stewart 1987b). So can the scholarly–imaginative process that sends analysts and analysands to look up the roots of a particular word in the appendix of a dictionary (Lockhart 1983), or do library research on the natural, historical and mythic origins of a particular image. Shared images and enactments (Mindell 1982, 1985; Schwartz-Salant 1984, p. 15; Dreifus 1987) can also be understood as forms of active imagination.

Stewart points out that active imagination and creative imagination are the same process. Both are expressed through 'rhythm,' 'ritual,' 'reason' and 'relationship' (1987b, pp. 138–42; 1987c). But creative imagination is turned to the creation of the cultural forms: art, religion, philosophy and society; active imagination is turned to the creation of the personality. This leads to a new understanding of active imagination as rhythm (dance/movement, sandplay, painting, poetry, sculpting, weaving, etc.), ritual (imagination of the sacred, inner voices, dialogue with the gods), reason (imagination of number and origins, cosmos and meaning, scholarly amplification), and relationship (empathic imagination, especially work with the transference and countertransference). As active imagination, rhythm, ritual, reason and relationship serve the psychological attitude and foster the development of self-reflective consciousness.

Although I am interested in all aspects of the analytic process, I am particularly drawn to understand and develop dance/movement as a form of active imagination. Movement is not of equal importance to everyone, but it may be essential for some. And it is helpful for many. The body grounds the limitlessness of the unconscious. Even so, there are those who are able to enter and interact with the imaginal world without getting up to move. I am comfortable with that because that is their way. I think what is more important to me nowadays than whether someone moves or not, is whether or not they are able to engage the imagination. There are many forms of active imagination. Each person has to find his or her best way.

As the process of individuation leads us to become who we are, certain analysts and analysands are inevitably led to use dance/movement as a part of their analytic work. For those with a 'motor imagination' (Jung 1938b, p. 474), dance/movement is simply the most immediate, natural way to give form to the unconscious. There are also those who find dance movement essential because they feel alienated from the body and now sense deeply that they must learn to listen to it.

DANCE/MOVEMENT AS ACTIVE IMAGINATION

Active imagination in movement involves a relationship between two people: a mover/analysand and a witness/analyst. It is within the relationship that the mover may begin to internalize the reflective function of the witness, i.e. to yield to the unconscious stream of bodily felt sensations and images, while at the same time bringing the experience into conscious awareness.

To begin, both mover and witness may participate in a brief warm-up period that usually involves gentle movements of bending, stretching and rotating. 'Pedestrian movement; simple walking, swaying, and running are all ways of breaking inertia and putting the body in motion' (Blom and Chaplin 1988, p. 57). Such easy movements release a kind of lubricating fluid to the joints and prepare the physical body for more activity. The warm-up may also serve as a rite of entry to active imagination; stretching, relaxing and attending to the depth and rhythm of one's breathing is the best way I know to open to the unconscious.

In their beautifully written book on dance improvisation, Blom and Chaplin (1988) suggest a lovely warm-up that plays with images of lubrication.

Start standing or lying down. Imagine a small puddle of oil in the palm of each hand. Move your hands around so the oil can get deep into the joints, muscles, knuckles, fingertips. Let the flow be easy, continuous, sinuous, no sudden starts or stops. Let the oiling proceed up through the wrist, lower arm, and elbow. Then onto the shoulders with smooth continuous movement. *Once one part of the body gets oiled, it continues to move in the same way*; it does not stop. Continue to oil the rest of your body with the sinuous motion. Once every part is in motion, keep the sustained flow and move a little faster, then faster still. Don't get jerky; keep the sense of ongoingness, no jolts or punctuation, just an overall, never-ending motion.

(Blom and Chaplin 1988, p. 58)

Different warm-ups are developed with different individuals, according to the needs of the moment. For example, a warm-up that emphasizes the smooth sense of ongoingness described above might be all wrong for the person who is attempting to give form to chaotic or explosive images. Or, parts or all of it might be just right for the person who wants to move, but would like some help

113

getting started. Sometimes, some of the people I work with will bring a record or tape and we will move together to music. Other times, I might choose a record that reflects and supports a particular mood. More often than not, though, we will warm-up in silence, doing simple movements, each with our own inner focus.

After the warm-up, the mover closes his or her eyes, attends inwardly and waits for an impulse to move, while the witness finds a corner in the room where s/he can sit and watch. At the beginning, the witness carries a larger responsibility for consciousness; the mover is simply invited to immerse in his or her own fluctuating rhythms of movement and stillness. The movement itself may take no more than ten minutes, or it can go on for half an hour or more. Sometimes it is helpful to decide in advance on a time period, something like ten, fifteen or twenty minutes, and have the analyst serve as timekeeper, letting the mover know when to (gradually) bring the movement process to an end.

In the early stages of the work, the mover may remember very little. But gradually, the mover learns to allow the movement to unfold and at the same time pays attention to what the body is doing. The mover also develops a more differentiated sense of where the movement comes from, i.e. the inner world of bodily felt sensations and images. When the mover is aware of both the expressive action and its sensory-imaginal source, s/he is likely to be conscious of the emotion or emotional tone as well. But it does not always happen that way. For example, the emotion may be strongly felt on a visceral level, but without awareness of the images that would give it meaning. On the other hand, there are movers who experience the unconscious as an inner landscape rich with mythic images, yet their relationship to it may be curiously detached, as if it had nothing to do with them. In time, active imagination in movement tends to develop in us a more differentiated, balanced relationship to both the sensory and imaginal aspects of our emotional life.

Physical safety issues need to be discussed. The mover closes his or her eyes in order to listen for the inner sensations and images. But if he or she begins any large swinging, spinning, leaping movement – any kind of momentum that could lead to a collision with windows, furniture, or what have you, it is essential that the eyes be open. Even when the quality of movement is smaller and slower, movers have to learn to open their eyes from time to time to keep an orientation to the room. It is difficult to do this without losing the inner-directed focus. But if the work involves a true meeting of conscious and unconscious, maintaining a sense of where one is in a room becomes part of the conscious standpoint. This is easy to say, but often extremely difficult to do. When one is moving in this way, the eyes usually *want* to stay closed. To open the eyes (even a tiny slit) takes a major effort. At times, the mover's eyes feel as if they are glued shut. But this struggle is an essential part of active imagination, that is, to develop the capacity to bear the tension of the opposites – to open fully to the unconscious while at the same time maintaining a strong conscious orientation.

In the midst of moving, people often remember a particularly vivid aspect of a dream, or an early childhood experience. For example, while moving low, close to the floor, an analysand suddenly remembered the full impact of what it was like when she fell and broke her leg at the age of six. In a seemingly random way, one of her legs had taken on a particular kind of twisted tension; the memory followed. This was the first time in recent years she remembered the painful, helpless, humiliating feelings that came as she tried to get up, but could not. These were exactly the feelings that had brought her into analysis. She felt unable to 'take a stand' or 'stand on her own two feet.' The process of active imagination in movement took her directly to the emotional core of the complex.

This brief description illustrates the vital link between memory and the moving body. It is as if certain memories are stored kinesthetically and can best be retrieved through the movements of the body. The great French novelist Marcel Proust wrote at length about this: 'Our arms and legs are full of sleeping memories of the past' (1928, p. 2). Sometimes the movements seem to be random. Other times, we discover that a particular posture or gesture is always there, no matter what we do we can't get away from it. But whether the movement that holds a particular memory appears randomly or consistently, it is our embodied link to the past.

It was very important for my analysand to retrieve such a long forgotten memory. Continuing work was needed to understand and integrate it on a more conscious level. Verbal dialogue and exchange was an essential part of the process. Through her dreams, fantasies, and exploration of feelings that arose in the transference relationship, we learned that the real problem was not the broken leg, rather it was a family atmosphere that could not tolerate feelings of helplessness, as if it were shameful to be in pain or to be in need of help.

People generally know when they want to move, but everyone

seems to approach it differently. Some move every hour; others only when they feel drawn to explore a particular theme in movement. Some move in the middle of the hour, with time for verbal exchange before and after. Others like to begin the hour with dance/movement. It may consist only of a brief warm-up as a way to become more fully present; then the person sits down and talks about whatever is on his or her mind. Or, the warm-up may lead into a deeply imaginative, emotional process that opens material for us to explore for the rest of the hour.

Chapter Fifteen

MOVEMENT THEMES, EGO AND SHADOW

Through the years I have noticed that certain similar patterns or themes emerge in the movement process of many individuals. Some of these appear and reappear with consistency and strength. In my opinion, these themes emerge from and draw attention to different aspects of the psyche.

Mary Whitehouse (1958) was the first dance therapist to describe movement from the perspective of conscious and unconscious. She identified intentional movement that is directed by the ego, unintentional movement that comes from the unconscious, and movement from the Self that unites both. She describes movement from the Self as 'the coming together of what I am doing and what is happening to me' (1958, p. 4). These simple yet profound ideas led to a new sensitivity about the origins of movement in the psyche.

Janet Adler (1973), who studied with Whitehouse, describes certain body level themes that emerge at a particular stage in the therapeutic process. These are: 1) Heightened attention to specific body parts; 2) movement patterns that are culturally understandable; and 3) idiosyncratic movements. In another paper, Adler (1987) differentiates between movement patterns that can be traced to personal history and those that seem to come from a transpersonal source.

Building on the contributions of Whitehouse and Adler, as well as my own observations, I shall speak about the sources in the psyche out of which movement can arise and describe the movement themes that seem to be associated with each. I offer this material as a contribution toward understanding the meaning of the vast assortment of movements that appear in active imagination.

The sources in the psyche listed below also show the developmental process that is recapitulated in analysis. We begin with the conscious position; regress to earlier stages of development as we experience the emotional core of our complexes; and then with the constellation of the ego-Self axis, we grow ourselves up again. With each cycle of regression and integration, we are able to put another piece of the past where it belongs and at the same time realize a new sense of identity that points to the future. Obviously, this is easier to say than to go through.

Movement reflects the total personality; it draws from both conscious and unconscious sources. For clarity, we shall discuss each of the sources of movement in the psyche separately. But in reality, there is a constant interplay between them.

I offer the following broad perspective on the origins of movement in the psyche. The sources listed below will provide a framework for our discussion:

1 Conscious, ego-directed movement
2 Movement from the personal unconscious
3 Movement from the cultural unconscious
4 Movement from the primordial unconscious
5 Movement from the ego-Self axis of identity

CONSCIOUS EGO-DIRECTED MOVEMENT

This broad category of movement includes every conscious, deliberate physical action. It includes the voluntary aspect of our gestures, body carriage, work actions and play. Conscious movement involves the intentional use of time [faster or slower, sudden or sustained], space [direct or flexible path], weight [firm or light touch] and flow [bound tension or unrestrained] (Laban 1971).

When we use dance/movement as a form of active imagination, the ego interweaves with and helps give form to movement impulses that come from the unconscious. It may also inhibit the expression of unconscious material that feels too painful, frightening, or overwhelming to come to conscious awareness. Either way, whether the ego fosters or inhibits the expression of unconscious content, the process reflects a dynamic interplay between conscious, deliberate physical action and movement that comes from the unconscious.

From a developmental perspective, ego-directed movement is first constellated at about 16–18 months of age, when the baby discovers that s/he has the ability to 'pretend.' As adults, an experience that corresponds to 'pretend' is full engagement in the symbolic process through free, imaginative use of mime. Mime is a highly conscious, nonverbal art form that uses body movement to mirror universal human experiences. It is a language that everyone understands. Our response to it is usually the spontaneous laughter of self-recognition.

In the early stages of analysis, movers frequently begin with the miming of a familiar behavior pattern that has served to ward off emotional pain. Inevitably, the imaginative process leads the mover directly to the emotional core of the underlying complex. The following descriptions are of three individuals, each in early stages of analytic work.

A man in his thirties begins to move by expressing a cheerful, extraverted, social attitude. He shakes hands, pours drinks, laughs, proposes toasts, but finally has to bid farewell to his guests. Left alone, his face and body sag. He sits heavily in a chair, lowers his head and grips it with his hands.

A woman in her early twenties dances as if she were a little girl seeking approval. She spins, smiles, and curtsies. She's charming and pretty as a Dresden doll, but there is a stiff, uncomfortable, unreal feeling to it all. As the dance continues, her eager-to-please attitude starts to fall away. The delicate gestures of her hands get sharper; gradually the sharpness and tension spreads through her body. Her hands now seem to be claws, her mouth looks contorted, her body has become twisted. She begins to breathe noisily and makes monstrous sounds as she scratches and tears at an invisible barrier that seems to surround her.

A busy, active executive enacts her over scheduled life. She looks at her watch frequently as she moves from one demanding task to another. For a moment she pauses, looks down to the ground and realizes how tired she is. She struggles briefly with her yearning to lie down, and overcomes it by returning to the portrayal of her active life.

(Chodorow n.d.)

Each person in his or her own way struggles with the tension between an overly bright, adaptive persona and its shadow. These portrayals are more conscious than not. But as shadow issues emerge, the movement qualities become more autonomous. As in any analytic process, a pair of opposites will be constellated. Out of the experience of that twofold tension, a third reconciling

119

symbol will eventually be born: a new inner attitude that contains yet also goes beyond both perspectives. But we are getting ahead of ourselves.

As shadow issues emerge, we are led to movement themes that come from the personal unconscious.

THE SHADOW – MOVEMENT FROM THE PERSONAL UNCONSCIOUS

In contrast to conscious movement, themes that emerge from the personal unconscious are difficult to identify, especially in the early stages of the work. But as the patterns are recognized and worked with, most can be traced to emotionally charged events in the past that for one reason or another could not be fully experienced at the time. When strong feelings cannot be felt, they split off and form the emotional core of a complex (see pp. 45–7).

I remember a woman who had been an abused child. In movement, no matter what she did, it turned violent. She pulled her own hair and then when she cried, she pounded at her head with her fists. When free movement leads the mover to recapitulate such a physically abusive experience, I may need to intervene. If so, I usually ask the person to pause or stop, so we can talk with each other. The critical question for me is whether the mover is actually hurting himself or herself. It is possible to express or enact even a brutal image, memory or feeling without causing physical pain or injury. Movement as active imagination is a symbolic process. Sometimes I have suggested the use of slow-motion movement, or the use of some tension instead of strength to express an image that might otherwise risk injury. Other times, I have suggested an exaggerated or stylized dance form that the mover is familiar with. There are also times when movement is simply not the best way to work with a particular complex.

Understanding the difference between literal and symbolic experience is of utmost importance. As movement patterns from the personal unconscious emerge, transference issues that reflect the parent/child relationship are likely to become prominent. The feelings, attitudes and complexes of the mover's parents tend to be transferred to the analyst as s/he watches the mover. As with any other analytic work, witnessing requires opening to the unconscious and at the same time maintaining a conscious analytic standpoint to reflect on the meaning of the symbolic action and the associated countertransference response.

120

Whether the complex movement patterns come from early childhood or from later stages of development, they have a form and/or meaning that is unique to the individual. Janet Adler was the first to write about them. She uses the word 'idiosyncratic' to describe these patterns:

> Idiosyncratic movements are most powerfully expressive of the true shadow – the darker, or unknown side – of the personality. They seem to have no meaning to anyone else, and appear unrelated to anyone else's movement patterns. Of its very nature, then, it is difficult to identify an idiosyncratic pattern as such until it is repeated so many times that it becomes clear. Even then I seldom have the slightest idea what it means or where its source lies.
>
> (Adler 1973, p. 48)

She describes an idiosyncratic (complex) pattern in the movement process of a young woman who is called 'Heather.'

> While lying on her side ... she lifted one leg straight up and then put it down, bent, foot flat on the floor in front of her other leg. She then pushed against the floor with her bent leg, pivoting her body around ninety degrees.
>
> (ibid., p. 48)

Adler goes on to describe how this pattern evolved into consecutive quarter turns, close to the ground, which took the mover into a brief but very frightening tantrum. Heather wrote in her journal: 'It's amazing how my body had remembered that motion where my mind had forgotten about it' (ibid., p. 48).

Janet Adler relates that this mover had frequent temper tantrums between the ages of 9 and 12. Now as a young adult, the movement process had taken her back to the emotional core of that complex. In the movement sessions she tried to stop or change the leg lifting, pushing and turning pattern, but found she couldn't get away from it. No matter what she did, free movement took her back to this idiosyncratic pattern which remained charged with unwanted feelings of rage and helplessness. As Heather became increasingly aware of her anger and of the many ways she consciously and unconsciously avoided it, she was able to recognize and talk more openly about a current life situation that was frustrating her. She also did a stamping angry dance that felt satisfying; it led to a spontaneous image of death and new life that was deeply reassuring to her. Finally, the leg lifting, pushing, turning pattern took her fully into and through a wild tantrum.

Heather had a second idiosyncratic pattern – unusually slow movement. At a certain point it led to the frightening feeling of immobility. She then remembered unhappy feelings that pervaded her childhood. This aspect of the family atmosphere had never been expressed or acknowledged. She now realized that the pre-adolescent tantrums had been her way to keep the immobilizing feelings of depression from taking over.

In addition to idiosyncratic movement patterns, specific parts of the body may be invested with repressed emotion. For example, some body parts carry heightened tension. Other parts may look and feel dead. There are also times when psychological pain is so unbearable that it converts to symptoms that cause physical discomfort instead. One way or another, a particular somatic condition draws attention to itself. If the mover can stay focused on the body part or symptom as it is, without trying to change it, the process of denial and repression may be reversed. A meaningful symbolic gesture may emerge along with feelings associated with the complex. When this happens, we see a symbol in the process of transformation, as it moves out of the personal unconscious and into an expressive form that is bearable and can be consciously understood.

Janet Adler (1973) illustrates such a process as she describes the heightened tension in Heather's hands and how they began to work with it.

> In the very first session her hands were obviously more tense than the rest of her body. She wrote in her journal: 'What was interesting was the more I tried to relax them, the tenser they got.' In the second session, when her hands were again exceptionally tense, I suggested she focus on them, let them go where they wanted to go, not try to make them relax. She was able to do this easily and soon her hands clasped tightly together, her entire body sank, and her face looked very sad. At the end of the experience she spoke briefly of a feeling of sadness. By the fifth session Heather's hands were clawing at herself, and she became aware of anger welling up beneath the sadness.
>
> (pp. 47–8)

I have touched on three of the movement themes described in Adler's study: 1) the leg lifting, pushing turning pattern; 2) the unusually slow movement; and 3) the heightened tension in the hands. A full review would go beyond the development I wish to address here. Janet Adler's papers are beautifully written and rich with detailed movement descriptions and reflections on their link with the therapeutic process. I recommend them to the reader who wishes to learn more about movement and the psyche.

It is clear that emotions expressed at the level of the personal unconscious derive from complexes. The themes are difficult to identify because the content has been repressed, and the nature of the expressive action is complicated. It is at this level of the psyche that we see the myriad emotional complexes that Stewart, building on Darwin and Tomkins, calls 'complex family emotions' (in press). These are mixtures and modulations of the innate affects that develop in the family.

For example, tantrums erupt out of a complex mixture of Rage, and a helpless quality that derives from Shame. Although Rage is prominent, the expressive action of a tantrum sometimes also includes a helpless kind of flailing about. The patterns that express depression seem to be a complex mixture of Sadness and Shame. Hatred is a complex mixture of Contempt and Anger. Individual complexes often include elements of the other fundamental emotions as well. Some of the other complex family emotions include guilt, greed, suspicion, deceit, jealousy, envy and the like; as well as mercy, compassion, courage, love, hope, generosity, admiration and the like (see above, p. 5 and p. 78).

From my own experience, movement that expresses the shadow, that is, the personal unconscious, can usually be identified by its seemingly random, complicated or murky qualities. Even when the theme becomes obvious, both mover and witness may be puzzled by where it comes from and what it means. Because of its idiosyncratic nature, movement from this level of the unconscious can be understood only through the associations and memories of the mover. The themes that emerge tend to be related to the family atmosphere (often experienced in the therapeutic relationship) and the complex family emotions.

As mover and witness are able to stay with the experience, the clear, recognizable expressive pattern of one or more fundamental emotions usually begins to emerge. Sometimes the emotion is in a state of primal intensity. Other times it feels more modulated, bearable and containable. Still other times, the expressive pattern is recognized as a symbolic cultural gesture. I will take these up in the next chapter.

Chapter Sixteen

MOVEMENT FROM THE CULTURAL UNCONSCIOUS

Expressive actions that can be culturally 'read' have their source in the cultural unconscious. At this level, symbolic actions emerge or even erupt spontaneously to the complete surprise of the mover. Many of the same actions, or similar ones, eventually come into the cultural collective as dance steps; ritual actions of prayer and worship; and social customs. There are even formal gestures that amplify scholarly arguments. Thus, the symbolic actions of the cultural unconscious are mirrored in the external cultural forms.

Piaget's contribution includes some lovely observations that demonstrate how the cultural attitudes are constellated in early childhood. The following selection is from a series he wrote on the development of his daughter, Lucienne. For Piaget, this series demonstrates Lucienne's acquisition of a new concept involving displacement of objects. For us, it shows the development of the imagination as well as the intellect. It includes a centering process and culminates in a dance.

At 1;3 (12) [1 year, 3 months, 12 days] she holds a branch of foliage in her hand. She detaches the leaves and throws them to the ground one by one. Each time she very carefully examines the trajectory. The same day she alternately moves a strainer away from her and brings it toward her.

The next day, at 1;3 (13) she uses the same strainer to elaborate an original group of displacements; she pivots about, and at each new position displaces the strainer in a corresponding arc after having first put it as far from her as possible. The strainer thus describes a wide circular movement around her, following her in its own rotation.

At 1;4 (8) her finger pushes blocks on a closed box and steers them to the edge until they fall.

At 1;4 (27) she studies the fall of a very light little feather which flutters as it falls. She repeats this experiment indefinitely.

At 1;4 (28) she carries a flower from one place to another (from a table to a sofa and vice versa). Lucienne prefaces this each time with a kind of dance step which she makes up herself.

(Piaget 1954, p. 211)

With adults too, the cultural unconscious holds a wide range of emotional expression that has a formalized quality. An example of this is shown in the movement process of a recently bereaved woman. She had no conscious awareness that Jewish tradition, as well as many others, requires the tearing of a garment or piece of cloth as a formal gesture of grief:

She wanted to move, but when she first began to attend inwardly, she became immobilized. The images that came were of self-destruction: hurling herself against the walls, tearing at her own flesh. She then shifted her attention from images to bodily sensations, and found that her heart felt as if it was tearing apart. As she stayed with the feeling of her heart being torn, her hands grasped at the sweatshirt she was wearing. Slowly, with a quality that can best be described as 'inevitable,' her hands began to tear through the cloth of her garment.

(Chodorow 1984, p. 44)

Active imagination in movement took this woman directly to the most ancient expressions of human anguish. On one hand, we seek to join the lost beloved person who is now dead; frantic actions of self-injury would lead to such a union in death, or to a living death of disfigurement, stigmata. On the other hand, when heart-rending images are culturally mirrored by tearing a piece of cloth, we can begin that painful grieving recognition of final separation.

One of the great gifts of Jung's psychology is, I think, the larger perspective it offers to the experience of suffering. In isolation, an individual's response to trauma may seem pathological. But with a larger cultural perspective, the personal pain of an individual becomes related in some way to the experience of all humankind. It does not take away the pain, but it can restore a quality of dignity to the most chaotic or despairing symptom.

As I have said above, the formal postures and gestures shown in art, religious rituals, philosophical discourse and social inter-actions originate in the cultural unconscious. So do the myriad cultural images of myth, legend and fairy tale. Once again we see the ongoing, interwoven relationship between action and image. Each potentiates the other.

When movement comes from the cultural unconscious, the mover often follows an ongoing stream of mythic imagery. Similar in certain ways to the mime-like enactments of conscious, ego-directed movement, the expressive actions of the cultural un-conscious tend to be clear and understandable. The ways they dif-fer have to do with the degree of spontaneity. Movement that comes out of the cultural unconscious tends to be unplanned; ego directed movement tends to be more planned, deliberate.

At the level of the cultural unconscious the mover is usually aware of the motivating images. These include interactions with every kind of interior landscape and the personified beings that appear. By in-terior landscape, I mean that sense of knowing that I am in a room doing active imagination, but at the same time I imagine myself to be in some other place. My movements reflect what it is like to move through the particular landscape as it appears before me. For example, if the imaginal sun is over bright, I am likely to find myself squinting and may shade my eyes. If I cross a stream, my movements are likely to reflect whether I take my shoes off and wade across, or balance on rocks and logs, or jump across it. If I wade, the move-ments of my face and body will probably show whether the water is ice cold or pleasantly warm; whether the stream bottom is sandy or full of stones; whether the stones are rounded and covered with moss, or whether they have sharp edges, and so forth.

If I come across a bird or fish or frog that wants my attention, my movements will reflect many details of the interaction. Most of the time I am likely to be myself, that is to say, remain in my own body as I interact with the images that appear. At the level of the cultural unconscious the images may be god-like or they may be human; I may interact with any kind of natural or mythic ani-mal image that appears; I may also be drawn to interact with spe-cial (that is, personified) plants and minerals.

There are also times when the images themselves seem to want to be embodied, as if the image could make itself better known by entering the body of the mover. When this occurs, the experience shifts from *dancing with* a particular image to allowing oneself to *be danced by* it.

An example of this follows: a middle-aged professional woman in analysis dreamed about a spider. In the dream, she was trying to kill the spider, or at least frighten it away. Instead, the spider jumped inside her clothes and rested on her right upper back. It was clear to her and to me when she talked about it in analysis that the spider represents something in the unconscious that the woman wants to get rid of. Typical of most complexes, the dreamer's direct attack caused it to retreat to a part of her psyche/ soma that she could not see. She couldn't see her back, but she could feel it there. The spider had a grip on her.

During that analytic hour in the midst of free movement, she noticed a painful spasm in her back that reminded her of the dream. Later on she wrote in her journal:

As I remembered the dream, my body immediately began a rolling, writhing, uncomfortable attempt to get the spider out of there. But it had a grip on me and wouldn't let go. Finally, as I reached for it with my left hand (it was still near my right shoulder blade), it released its hold. I paid close attention to it, as it slowly and deliberately crawled down my right arm. I finally held it in my hands, making a cupped space for it.

Then I seemed to become the spider. I crouched and wrapped my arms around my legs and ankles. I felt like a predator in the center of my web – waiting. I held a long silk thread which I could pull, to capture something.

Then I was myself again and the spider began to grow until it was bigger than I. It loomed over me. It got to be so dark that I wondered whether I might be inside its body. Then my mind wandered – and suddenly I was outside again, but now my hands were bound together by strong spider's silk. My first response was passive and disconnected. But as I gradually realized the degree of restriction, a sense of urgency built. I started to roll and struggle and bite at my bonds until I was free.

After I freed my wrists, I rocked with my arms loosely crossed, and knelt toward the earth. I then found my way toward the wall, and found the spider there, tiny again, as in the dream. I invited it into my hand and sat with it while it grew to the same size as I. We sat together and I tried to sense what it wanted. I lay under it now and saw a stinger come out of its body to sting me. I struggled to keep that from happening. Then I understood that the poison I feared was more like a vaccine. I lay down and let the spider sting me. It penetrated my lower left abdominal quadrant. I felt it go inside and also felt both areas of my body charged with energy – my upper back (on the right) and my lower front (on the left).

My analysand was struggling to come to terms with issues related to the Great Mother, also known as Spider Woman, Spinning Woman, Maya, the weaver of illusions, and many other names. On an everyday level, unrealistic attitudes of dependency usually stem from a mother complex. On a conscious or unconscious level, we expect the world to be the good mother that will take care of us – we may be resentful, even enraged because it is not. Recognizing the cold-blooded, predator aspect of the Great Mother is necessary to any deep psychological development. To recognize it in Her is to also recognize that unwanted, rejected aspect of our own nature.

In most of the movement sequence (as in her dream) the mover/analysand interacted with the spider while remaining herself. But at a certain point in the movement, she embodied the spider and experienced on a deep immediate level something that she had to learn about the nature of the dark feminine (Perera 1981). This mover had recently suffered an enormous personal loss. She was now forced to recognize and come to terms with certain illusions that previously had led her to see life as she wished it to be, rather than the way it is. Ultimately, she submitted to the spider's poison-like sting. In permitting a penetration by the dark spider, she was led into and through a period of deep mourning and eventually to a new integration of the opposites in herself.

I shall close this discussion of movement from the cultural unconscious with a narrative written by a young woman. Wyman (1978) reports that the mover is in her mid-twenties and involved in a deep process of movement psychotherapy. Since the movements of the body are not described in detail, I encourage the reader to take the time to pause and reflect on what the movement process might look like, given the mover's description of the landscape and the variety of mythic images that she interacts with:

I am on an island and want to get to shore where I see people playing and taking off their bathing suits. I see a boat tied up to my island. I untie it, get in and begin to row towards shore. The oar breaks. I can't make it. I rest and go to sleep in the boat as it drifts. Then I wake up, and jump out of the boat into the water. I meet a large pink fish (an angel fish?) under the water.

Later, I meet a golden catfish, who looks like a man with long whiskers. I get some gills so that I can stay under the water. I want to go to the grotto where I see all the old wise fish gathering. The catfish that I met earlier comes out. He tells me that I must go and play first. I join the little fish and we begin to play together. Suddenly a huge white light from above penetrates the sea above me. I look up. It is coming from a statue of the Virgin Mary. I am afraid to look. I look and under my gaze it grows larger and looms over me. I am very frightened. Slowly I begin to make my way up the steps of the altar. As I do, the statue begins to shrink, until it is a small twelve-inch statue. I pick it up and cradle it in my arms. I hold her to my breast and say 'I love you.' Then I toss her against the wall and she shatters. There is terror in my body. Once more I return to the water. I make my way to shore easily now. When I get there I lie on my back in the sand. The water washes over me, there is a feeling of dissolving. Then the floor turns into a huge mouth. It is devouring me. I am terrified and begin to cry.

(Wyman 1978, p. 83–4)

After dance/movement it is often helpful to ground the experience in some other form. In this situation, the young woman went to an area where art materials are available and gave form to her experience in clay. She made three figures. Later on, she wrote in her journal:

Many times I destroyed these figures, but each time I began to rework the clay, they reappeared. The figures are: a devouring mother, a hermaphrodite, and an old woman giving birth to an infant daughter.

(ibid., p. 84)

Chapter Seventeen

MOVEMENT FROM THE PRIMORDIAL UNCONSCIOUS

At the deepest level of the primordial unconscious we find the innate affects in a state of primal intensity: Ecstasy, Excitement, Anguish, Terror, Rage, Disgust/Humiliation and Startle. Emotional expression at this level can be so intense that there is little awareness of individual history or cultural meaning. Here the individual is engulfed by a primal emotion and may become merged with it.

Movement events that come out of such depths have a numinous effect on both mover and witness. The movement quality is autonomous, involuntary. Wordless vocalization usually accompanies physical action. Such sounds as laughing, crying out, sobbing, moaning, gasping, shouting, snarling, sneering and even gagging may be part of the movement process. It may last only a few moments or it may go on for a longer time. Deep sobbing sometimes goes on and on; also rolling, rollicking laughter.

The expressive action is most often overt, cathartic:

At a peak moment we leap or jump with Joy. We laugh. Our arms open wide as we experience an all embracing quality of infinite love, bliss, rapture.

In a moment of extreme Excitement we may stutter and stumble over our own feet. We are fascinated and engaged with every detail of an ever changing world. Even one's own body seems novel as we turn ourselves around, this way and that, even upside-down, to look at every new aspect of everything we see.

In Anguish, we cry and cry. There seems to be no end to it.

In a moment of Terror, time seems to stop. With heart pounding, muscles trembling, shoulders hunched, the mover is transfixed by impending disaster.

In Rage we feel a surge of explosive energy, heat and tension. Some people literally see red. Eyes are fixed, nostrils dilate, lips are open and show clenched teeth. We want to bite, hit, kick or strike out in any way we can.

In Disgust, lips curl, noses wrinkle. We pull away from a dirty, smelly object. In Humiliation we writhe and squirm and may even retch, because the dirty, smelly object we want to get away from is ourself. Convulsive movements from the middle of the body are typical of this toxic affect.

Startle is the primal response to our own disorientation. Something unexpected has happened, but we do not yet know what it is. Small startles often come in the midst of movement, as if to direct the mover's attention to a particular passing memory, thought or fantasy. There are also larger, sudden movements that are completely spontaneous and very intense. These seem to jolt the mover, particularly when in the midst of an undifferentiated, disoriented state.

When a primal affect erupts in the midst of movement, the emotion is so intense that it may take over completely, interrupting the imaginative process. There are also times when the imaginative process is so strong that it takes the mover to and through even the deepest affect. For example, we begin to sob (or rage, or tremble, or convulse), but the motivating image is so compelling that it feels as if we cannot stop. The sobbing (or other cathartic expression) is contained by the imaginative movement process and goes on within it. More often than not, though, the mover is stopped when a primal affect is constellated.

I am reminded of a movement therapy session many years ago with a woman who responded to her own emerging sensuality with the laughter of self-recognition. Then the laughter became so intense that everything else was absorbed into it. I shall include a description of the entire session to offer a sense of how she came to it, how it at first overwhelmed her and how we worked with it.

Teresa had been in individual dance/movement psychotherapy for nine months, attending weekly sessions. She had also been in verbal psychotherapy for several years before. She came into the studio this day and began to move immediately with a rhythmic side-to-side swaying. Her eyes closed as her head, shoulders and arms descended toward the ground. She gradually sank on to the floor where she lay quietly with a quality of absolute stillness, beautifully centered and concentrated. Then she began to move. At first she moved slowly. But she became increasingly free, loose and spontaneous. As it built in momentum, she was drawn upward, on to her feet. Her movements did not look dangerous in

131

themselves, but she got to be so unrestrained that I found myself moving around the room just in case she needed a protective 'buffer' between herself and cabinet edges or other obstructions. As I reflected on this afterwards, I realized I might have witnessed her without moving around the room to protect her. I might have said 'open your eyes,' – or she might have bumped into a wall or piece of furniture and we could have worked with her experience, that is: What it is like to feel free, spontaneous, unrestrained – and then be suddenly stopped? But in this particular session, I responded spontaneously in a protective, nurturant way. Teresa tended to be so harshly critical of herself that saying something like 'open your eyes,' or letting her bump herself against something did not feel useful.

After she experienced the loose, free quality for a long time, she was drawn again down toward the ground. She began to move slowly and sensuously on the floor, folding and unfolding her whole body. This led to a gentle smile of pure pleasure that flowed into soft laughter from time to time. After a while, the laughter became stronger. It took on a life of its own. The sensuous quality was replaced by a laughter that convulsed and rocked her entire body. This second type of laughter went on and on. She rolled on the floor, holding her belly as she laughed. I too was smiling and laughing. After a while I intervened and asked her to take whatever time she needed to come back. Up to this point she had allowed internally generated impulses to move her for nearly forty-five minutes.

As she gradually returned to everyday consciousness, her entire attitude changed. She became tense, negative, and strongly judgmental toward the parts of herself that had just emerged. Her first words were in a shocked and shaken voice: 'Wow, I really got pretty far out there!' We then talked together about the contrast between her emerging freedom of choice, spontaneity, sensuality; and the relative rigidity of her lifelong beliefs and lifestyle. Although she was increasingly able to acknowledge the tension between her two viewpoints, she continued to identify with the most familiar part of herself and maintained an attitude of self-condemnation.

We agreed to role play these two aspects of her personality. First we moved together, both enacting a harsh, judgmental quality. It was a stylized version of herself as a somewhat critical, controlled, respectable matron. Then I asked her to continue the same quality while I began to move similarly to the ways she had moved before. As my momentum began to build, I allowed myself to become genuinely less controlled, and she had to find a way of dealing with me. At first, she seemed to ignore me. However, she soon started to move around the edges of the studio, gently protecting me from bumping into obstructions, just as I had done for her earlier. When I moved into some of the pleasurable sensuality she had shown before, she was able to watch me, conveying a tentative sense of validation and acceptance. Then she joined me and we improvised together. Her movements now had a completely new kind of integration, a balance of freedom and control. So did mine. We ended after a brief, mutual, verbal exchange.

Teresa continued to consolidate this more integrated sense of herself. Questions of freedom and control stem from different personal experiences. They also carry the power of an issue that is common to all humankind. Although our work was clearly focused on Teresa's therapy process, I too experienced change. We were both affected by the primal power of her laughter and continue to reflect on its meaning for each of us individually and perhaps its meaning for all women.

And then there are times when an affect of primordial intensity is stirred or even constellated, but the mover keeps it contained. Instead of cathartic release, movement and sound are minimal; there are subtle but deeply felt changes in muscle tension, breathing and/or body temperature. If the mover can stay conscious and attentive to the inner experience, there is likely to be a shift at some point and more often than not a spontaneous release into laughter or tears.

There are also times when a primal affect seems to be constellated, but the mover is dissociated from it. When this happens, the movement may take on an emotionally strangulated, trance-like quality. Such dissociated affect may represent certain difficult or even devastating experiences from the pre-verbal, pre-symbolic developmental period of infancy. Pre-verbal memories are vivid when we are able to pay attention to them; they manifest in both sensory and imaginal realms. But it is difficult to retrieve them because there are no words available to organize and describe the event.

I remember a mover who began to get in touch with a gaping, empty feeling that was familiar to her. She imagined herself as a baby lying in a hospital crib. She had in fact been hospitalized for several weeks when she was four or five months old. In the movement, she imagined what it might have been like, and felt a wave of despair as she sensed that no one was there for her. She then lay very still for a long time, in an extremely withdrawn state. As I watched her, I first picked up a sense of infant-like movement that felt uncomfortable. But I could not imagine in my usual way. Then at a certain point I just went blank. After a while some part of me realized I was not paying attention, but I still could not figure out what I was feeling or what the mover's withdrawn state might be about, or where my attention had gone. Finally, I just let myself imagine around the image of blankness. It is empty. Nothing. Vacant. No one there. As I let myself relate to the blankness, the void, I began to feel a deep sense of sadness and loss.

The witness often picks up something of the mover's dissociated affect through the countertransference response. Sometimes it comes as a rush of intensely felt emotion; other times, as I described above, both mover and witness share a similar state of dissociation. When that happens, there may be nothing to do but be in it together and talk with each other about it at a later time. If we can muster a bit of observing ego, the primordial images themselves will lead us to experience the emotion. Getting interested in the images and imagining what they are about is the best way I know to work with a state of dissociation. In my experience, images related to the *void*, the *abyss, chaos, alienation* and *disorientation* frequently underlie a state of dissociated affect (see pp. 82–3)

As far back as Aristotle, catharsis has been described in two ways: 1) *Purging* or release of emotional tension and 2) *Purification* or transformation of emotional tension (n.d. pp. 313–14). The value of purging is that it offers immediate relief of tension. It can also be of great value to the individual who feels shut down from the spontaneous, fully embodied expression of deep affect. The value of purification involves the development of a certain kind of ego control as well as relief through suppression and sublimation of the emotion. This may be especially valuable to the individual who has experienced little differentiation between impulse and action. The danger of an over-emphasis on purging is that we simply get to be good at it. The danger of a one-sided emphasis on purification is that by avoiding the deepest affects, we avoid life. In my experience, when either form of catharsis is idealized, there is little or no fundamental change. Psychological development requires an interweaving of both.

Chapter Eighteen

MOVEMENT FROM THE EGO-SELF AXIS

Movement from the ego-Self axis has a different quality. Many of the patterns are spiral or geometric in form with a strong central axis that seems to balance and counterbalance all the dynamic pairs of opposites possible in a moving body. It is as if the mover is being moved by the ordering and centering process of the psyche. These experiences tend to come as a constellation of the Self at critical stages in the work.

Rhythmic fluctuations are often prominent. Sequential rhythmic movement can interweave such opposite elements as above and below, right and left, advance and retreat, etc. For example, a mover had been feeling stuck for a long time as she struggled with the seemingly irreconcilable demands of two inner figures. She had often been taken over by moods that seemed to express one or the other of them. She also experienced a kind of torment at times, as if she were being pulled apart by the inner conflict. One day in movement, she finally paused and stood between them. She began what at first looked like a kind of random weaving pattern. It developed into her turning first to one and then to the other, with alternating, inward gathering gestures of her right arm and then her left. As she did this, a soft, rebounding rhythm began to shift her weight from one foot to the other and led both arms to simultaneously shape a very round, three-dimensional figure eight (on its side). She laughed as she recognized a moving symbol of infinity. The emotional change was from helplessness and tears, to a competent, energized, even playful new experience of herself.

Movement from the ego-Self axis can usually be recognized by the fully-dimensional way that the body moves in space. I remember an hour when a man began standing and then slowly lifted his arms high. At first, his body attitude was flat, two-dimensional, as if limited to a lateral plane. Then, led by his own curiosity, he began to rotate his upper torso as far as it would go to one side and then the other. What he discovered was the wonderful, diagonal counter-tension that we humans can feel between our four large ball and socket joints (shoulders and trochanters). Once he felt the counter-tension, he became even more involved and began to play with it, find out what he could do with it. For the next ten or twelve minutes, he was completely absorbed in a fully embodied exploration of every dimension. He seemed to shape and carve the space around him, his balance was firm yet flexible, his movement path was mainly in spirals. He is not a professional dancer, but his movement was the essence of rhythmic harmony.

Carolyn Grant Fay describes such an experience. The mover is a woman who has had many years of analytic work:

I lay for what seemed like a long time, listening inwardly to myself. My throat brought itself to my attention. It hurt and felt constricted and tense, so I let my throat lead me into movement. It led me up to kneeling, then forward, and then slowly across the floor in a sort of crouching position. In my imagination I became aware as I concentrated on the throat that it was red with blood. The heart area was also aching and bloody. Finally my throat brought me up to standing and propelled me farther along. It stopped me suddenly, and I just stood there. At this point I collapsed onto the floor and lay there motionless. There was no movement ... not an image ... nothing.

After a while I became aware that the color red from the blood was there at my throat and breast. Little by little it became many shades of red from light pink to deep crimson. A rose began to take shape, rising out of the throat and heart through movements of my arms up, out, and around. The rest of my body down from that area seemed, in the fantasy, to be forming the stem and leaves of the flower. All sorts of superlatives come to me now as I try to express how I felt at that moment: warm, happy, fulfilled, in order, at one with myself.

(Fay 1977, pp. 26–7)

The mover reflects on the meaning of this part of the fantasy/ movement.

The collapse onto the floor, and the nothingness that followed, seemed to symbolize a death of what had been wounded. I think of a dream I had ... in which a woman, bleeding at the throat and breast, and ragged and grey from centuries of neglect, appeared. I associated this woman to myself at eighteen when my mother died. The reawakening to the color and the forming of the rose, with all the concomitant feelings of well-being, I associated with rebirth.

(Fay 1977, p. 27)

In analysis, movement from the ego-Self axis is usually preceded by a difficult period of woundedness, inner conflict, a life crisis. As reported above, it may be experienced as a death and rebirth. The mythic image is the *Mandala*, a union of opposites that expresses the totality of the Self. The constellation of the ego-Self axis is a developmental event that unites conscious and unconscious in a new way and offers a new experience of one's self, a new sense of identity. We cannot will it to happen, but when it occurs, we recognize it and feel grateful.

The following narrative was written by a woman who had recently experienced the death of a loved one. The movement experience did not end her grief, rather it seemed to offer a compensatory glimpse of wholeness and hope in the midst of a very dark time.

My left hand became hard fisted. It was like a phallus. I moved through all levels with this strong, hard, left forearm and fist. Then the fist opened. It opened so slowly that it was like a reversal from numbness. As my hand relaxed slowly into openness, a large diamond appeared in my palm. It was heavy. I began to move my left arm in slow spirals around myself. I was aware of feeling the sequential, overlapping rotations of shoulder, elbow, wrist, and even fingers. Both arms came to stillness together, joined behind my back. The left hand continued to hold the diamond. Then the image of the diamond came in front of my eyes. It grew larger, until I could see through it with both eyes. It showed me a vision of everything broken up by its facets. The diamond grew larger, until I was inside it looking out. The light was bright – almost golden. I bathed in it and felt that it was a healing kind of light. Now my body shape took on the diamond's many facets. I was myself, my own shape, but each part of me had many cut surfaces. It was as if I could 'see' through the myriad facets of all of me. There was a sense of wonder and suspension and peacefulness.

(Chodorow 1986, p. 94)

I will close with a series of psychotherapy sessions that led to a sequence of movement from the ego-Self axis. The mover, Sara, is a gifted psychotherapy student in her early thirties. She too, recently suffered a profound, personal loss that made her painfully aware of her tendency to deny the life of her own body. In previous work with movement, she yearned toward the sky, as if barely touching the earth with her feet. In her grief, she discovered that her feet were connected to the ground. The early sessions involved a lot of walking, just feeling the ground under her feet. Soon the rest of her body followed her awareness downward, on to the floor. For the next several months, whenever she moved, she remained intimately connected to the ground, rolling, crawling, creeping, crouching and rocking. She moved through a lot of grief and began to express other feelings as well. Memories came of feeling hatred, rage, fear and lack of support. Throughout this time she became increasingly aware of sensations in her pelvis, and movement began to initiate from her pelvic floor. Different images began to accompany this new way of moving.

One image was of blood coming out of her hip joints. She experienced this as a pouring forth of life-blood – an image of both woundedness and healing. In the movement enactment she spread it all over herself, outside and in, drinking, swallowing, absorbing. Then, covered with blood, she descended into some caverns. Her pelvis was so alive, it led the rest of her body. Light came out of her pelvis, enabling her to see where she was going. At the bottom of the cavern, there was a pool of mud. She bathed in the mud and felt grounded, connected, secure.

That night she dreamed that her grandmother gave her a sum of money in the form of 'securities.'

In the next session, all of her movement centered on pelvic initiation. Finally, she simply sat on the floor with legs outstretched, as if she and the earth were one. The way she sat expressed a primal quality of strength and groundedness. From this sitting, there grew a slow but increasingly compelling rhythmic pattern. Her arms, head, and torso began to move as a unit, tracing a half-circle through horizontal space, right to left, counterclockwise. When her body could go no further in the horizontal plane, it shifted to the lateral plane and she completed another half-circle: this one left to right, clockwise, over her own head, like a rising and setting sun. When she could go no further to her right (in the lateral plane), she began the cycle again, by returning to the horizontal, counterclockwise sweep. She repeated the cycle over and over with strong rhythmic shifts and a wonderful clarity of spatial intent. Her movement was an integration of two half-circles: one counterclockwise, the other clockwise. She also brought together two planes and four directions, creating a multidimensional, circular cross. It was a union of opposites in motion.

STAGES IN THE DEVELOPMENT OF THE EGO-SELF AXIS

Dance/movement is one of the most direct ways to reach back to our earliest experiences. Movers frequently lie on or move close to the ground. By attending to the world of bodily-felt sensations, the mover recreates a situation that is in many ways similar to that of an infant who swims in a sensory-motor world. The presence of the analyst/witness enables re-enactment and re-integration of the earliest pre-verbal relationship(s). It is here that images of the transference and countertransference may be most clearly recognized. At this level, the material touched may be experienced as toxic, even life threatening. At one time it may well have been that. But it is also at this level that we find the essential earliest stages of healthy, normal development.

The five symbolic events that I will describe are among those that appear and reappear in the movement process of many individuals. There were many years when I recognized the power of these patterns, but I did not know what to make of them. The movers had very little to say about them, but some sensed they had to do with early development – doing something essential for themselves now that had not been completed back then. I too, sensed that they might be enactments or re-enactments of early passages. But the major developmental theories I was aware of at the time emphasized pathology. It was obvious that these have a very different quality. As I understand them now, they represent stages of developing consciousness through the pre-verbal, pre-symbolic developmental period of infancy, i.e. from birth to approximately sixteen months (Stewart and Stewart 1979). I outlined these symbolic actions and interactions in the chapter on child development: 1) patterns of uroboric self-holding; 2) seeking the face of the witness and when found, a smile of recognition; 3) the laughter of self-recognition; 4) disappearance and reappearance; and 5) full engagement in the symbolic process via free imaginative use of mime. I will discuss each theme as it appears in dance/movement.

Uroboric: patterns of self-holding

Movers tend to explore a very wide range of uroboric self-holding. We see all kinds of patterns: one hand holding the other; thumb-holding; arm(s) wrapping around the torso to hold rib(s), elbow(s), hip(s), knee(s), foot or feet. All of these seem reminiscent of those earliest body experiences when we at first unintentionally find, then lose, then find again – and gradually discover what it is to hold and be held.

When the mover is immersed in self-holding, his or her eyes are closed, or have an inward focus. There is usually rocking, swaying or some other kind of rhythmic pulsation. The quality is usually complete self-containment. If the analyst/witness opens him or herself to a state of *participation mystique*, s/he may join the mover in a timeless state, and experience a similar kind of self-containment. If the analyst/witness does not enter into a state of *participation mystique* with the mover, s/he may feel excluded, irritated, uneasy – or shy, embarrassed to watch an experience of such intimate union with self. A wide range of responses may arise. When working with such early themes the countertransference response offers essential, vivid information about the analyst, the analysand and their relationship.

At times, the experience has a different, perhaps more conscious quality. There is a sense of wonderment as the mover's hands discover and explore the shape of his or her own body. As the mover's hands shape themselves to the bulges and the hollows, the hard bones and the soft flesh, there is a profound sense of self-recognition – as if meeting oneself for the first time. Both mover and witness often feel as if they are participants in an ancient ritual form. After many years of witnessing women and men spontaneously discovering the shape of their own bodies with their hands, I learned of a myth that demonstrates so clearly such a return to our uroboric origins. The myth of Changing Woman, who presses and molds her own body as she comes of age, is still re-enacted throughout the American Southwest in the form of an initiation ceremony.

The initiation ceremony is called the Kinaaldá by the Navaho. The Apache call it the Sunrise Dance (Quintero 1980). It is an elaborate ritual – a time of rejoicing to mark a girl's onset of menstruation. Her passage to womanhood is announced to the whole community in a dramatic four night ceremony.

Changing Woman had a miraculous birth and grew to maturity

in four days. At this time she had her first menstrual period. The Holy People were living on the earth then, and they came to her ceremony and sang songs for her. She originated her own Kinaaldá. One of the most important parts of the ceremony was molding her body. Some say that at the first Kinaaldá, Changing Woman molded her own body. The pressing or molding was done to honor the Sun and the Moon. Changing Woman was molded into a perfect form.

When the first-born human girl became Kinaaldá, Changing Woman did the same things for her. She pressed and molded the young woman's body, thus gifting her with beauty, wisdom, honor and self-respect. The Kinaaldá is part of the Blessing Way Ceremony. It is done today as it was done in the beginning (Frisbie 1967; Henderson 1985/1986; Sandner 1979, pp. 122–32; Quintero 1980).

First smile: recognition of the other (approx. 2nd month)

The movement process frequently evokes a special smile that is reminiscent of the infant's earliest recognition of the 'other.' When the movement comes to an end, it is almost always followed by continued inner attentiveness – a period of natural self-containment similar to the uroboric quality. Then, as the mover makes the transition to everyday consciousness, it is as if s/he is gradually waking up. When the mover's eyes open, s/he usually begins to search the room for the analyst. When the analyst's face is found, there is a mutual sense of reconnection and, most often, the smile(s) of recognition. The mover may have just experienced painful emotions; his or her face may still be wet with tears. But as s/he gradually comes back to the everyday world and scans the room for the analyst's face, there is a meeting and a clear-eyed smile.

First laugh: recognition of the self (approx. 3rd month)

From time to time, usually in the midst of movement, the mover laughs. There are many kinds of laughter. This one expresses joy in the sheer exuberance of bodily motion. There are also times when a particular image appears, and the mover laughs. The image may come in the midst of movement or stillness. Sometimes the mover has paused; it may also happen when the mover is feeling stuck. But with the laughter, something shifts. Afterwards, when it has occurred to me to ask about it, more often than not the mover laughs again and tells me about a kitten or dog or other kind of animal. Sometimes a particular animal (usually a pet) appears many times to the same mover. As we learn to listen to the body and follow what it wants to do, it seems natural that our animal instincts appear in a form we can live with – and we laugh.

Disappearance and reappearance: object constancy (approx. 9th month)

There are so many ways that the mover/analysand hides from the witness/analyst – and reappears. The dance/movement structure itself is a game of disappearance and reappearance – as the mover's eyes close and open again. But within the movement, even with eyes closed, the mover may turn away and do some small, intricate gestures that the witness cannot see. If the witness follows his or her curiosity and moves to a part of the room where the gestures can be seen, the mover may turn away again, and the cycle can repeat itself. Often, if the witness stays put, the mover turns around again to where s/he may be seen. Sometimes peek-a-boo and other hiding games and activities emerge as overt, central, conscious themes in dance/movement enactment.

Pretend play: separation of the world parents (approx. 16 months)

In the infant's life, this passage to conscious awareness of the symbolic world does not come through the word. Rather it comes through the discovery of nonverbal, symbolic play – that is, the baby discovers that s/he can pretend. In infancy as in analysis, this quality of movement is expressed through mime-like enactments. This brings us full circle because I described this quality of movement in the beginning. With this passage we are led as if for the first time to conscious, ego-directed movement.

I want to point out that the pre-verbal passages we have been discussing are expressed spontaneously in chairs as well as in dance/movement improvisation. For example, the patterns of self-holding and the self-contained rhythmic pulsations that I have described in relation to the uroboric stage may be part of any analytic experience that involves regression to that early time. As I remember the New York subway, a good deal of uroboric self-holding seems to go on there too. What I am trying to say is that it is not limited to analysis either. Similarly, the genuine smile that recognizes the face of another, the laughter of self-recognition, all kinds of subtle peek-a-boo interactions, as well as mime – are natural modes of expression and communication. These nonverbal expressive actions often underlie and punctuate spontaneous verbal dialogue and exchange.

Chapter Nineteen

CLOSING THOUGHTS

Looking back to the earlier chapters I described my development as a dancer and dance teacher, which led to the study of dance therapy and its practice. This was followed by continuing psychological studies and practice as a Jungian analyst. Central to my own development has been the constant awareness of the intertwining of body, psyche and the emotions. In the middle and later chapters I discussed the importance of the emotions, presented a theory that has oriented my work as a therapist, and illustrated the various levels of the psyche which are expressed through dance/movement. In this final chapter I look at the larger context of psychotherapy and analysis, with particular attention to the nonverbal expressive aspects. I will begin with Jung's view of the therapeutic relationship and the stages of therapy, then explore the value to clinical practice of a differentiated understanding of the emotions. I will close with a reflection on the experience of the witness.

PSYCHOTHERAPY AS A DIALECTICAL RELATIONSHIP

For Jung, psychotherapy is a real relationship between two human beings. He sat across from his patients, so that they could see his face and body and know what he was feeling. This is in contrast to Freud who tried to make the work impersonal by sitting behind the couch where his patients could not see him. When therapist and patient can see and be seen by each other, psychotherapy re-institutes the mirroring that is so fundamental to the parent-infant relationship. A natural fluctuation occurs between inner attention, and attention to the presence of the other. A couch is sometimes useful, but it is not essential to a state of reverie. At any time, the patient may lean back in a chair (or lie

144

on the floor), close his or her eyes and speak out loud without censoring.

STAGES OF PSYCHOTHERAPY

Jung differentiates four stages of psychotherapy for which he uses the 'somewhat unusual terms': 1) confession, 2) elucidation, 3) education, and 4) transformation (Jung 1931b, p. 55). Experience teaches that different people have different needs regarding psychotherapy.

The first stage, 'confession,' can be compared to confession in the religious tradition. Jung refers to 'the extraordinary significance of genuine, straightforward confession – a truth that was probably known to all the initiation rites and mystery cults of the ancient world' (ibid, p. 59). When such a cultural custom is alive and full of meaning, it functions as a vast, collective, psychotherapeutic system. But when it no longer works, people may turn to psychotherapy. The confession stage of psychotherapy involves a patient speaking freely and a non-intrusive therapist who listens. On a movement level, the patient moves freely in the presence of a therapist/witness. Janet Adler describes this quality of authentic movement as an immediate expression of how the individual 'feels at that moment. The spontaneous urge to move or not to move is not checked, judged, criticized, or weighed by the conscious mind' (Adler 1973, p. 43).

Jung points out that for some people, confession may be all that is needed. They feel better, express their appreciation, say goodbye, and go on with their lives. But for many, confession alone is not enough. Jung's second stage of psychotherapy, 'elucidation,' may then be necessary. Jung relates this stage to Freud's contribution. It basically involves working with and clarifying the underlying issues that come up in the transference. The patient becomes aware that s/he projects all kinds of unconscious complexes onto the therapist. With the therapist's help, s/he comes to understand these complexes. In movement, the work at this level goes on when the mover realizes s/he feels inhibited from moving freely in the presence of the witness. The mover gradually becomes aware of his or her fantasies about what the witness is thinking, feeling or doing. Expressing the fantasies and exploring their meaning are an important part of the work. It is also at this stage that the mover becomes aware of his or her movement repertoire and specific themes begin to appear and re-appear.

With reductive interpretations and the retrieval of memories from childhood that had been repressed, certain underlying issues may be cleared up and the patient may feel ready to end therapy. However, even with this understanding of fundamental issues, many people feel the need to continue into Jung's third stage of psychotherapy, 'education.' Jung relates this work to the contribution of Alfred Adler. Although Jung does not spell it out, he seems to suggest that this stage involves the development of a new social attitude, which was Adler's view of the end goal of psychotherapy. The stage of 'education' helps the person make a bridge from psychotherapy to life. The emphasis is on fostering new experiences. In movement, a similar process involves the discovery of a wider range of movement experiences. In realizing a wider choice of movement behavior, the task is to link these new resources to everyday life situations.

Jung's first three stages of psychotherapy reflect a more or less traditional psychotherapeutic approach. Hilde Bruch's clear, concise text for psychiatric residents and other student therapists presents three somewhat similar tasks that are basic to short term as well as long term therapy:

> In every form of psychotherapy several processes go on simultaneously and serially: by *listening* effectively to what the patient has to say, you may make him feel he has been heard and understood; by summarizing and *reformulating* what you have heard, you may help him take the first steps toward clarifying and reducing the underlying confusion that complicates his life; finally, by a more objective assessment of his resources and by *presenting alternatives*, you may help him arrive at a point where he can take action, no longer so helplessly caught in his anxieties and victimized by circumstances.
>
> (Bruch 1974, p. ix)

Whether the therapeutic process is described as confession, elucidation, education, or listening, reformulating, presenting alternatives – some people find a continuing process of inner work a necessity. This involves Jung's fourth stage of psychotherapy, 'transformation,' which is his particular contribution to the field. Work at this level draws the individual into a lifelong creative process called individuation. Individuation is the process of becoming one's self through the development of an ongoing, self-reflective, psychological attitude – 'Know Thyself.' This process may affect not only the patient, but the therapist too. Transformation involves a descent by both analyst and analysand 'into the soup,' so to speak, where the psyche of each has a profound influence on the other. The transformation stage of Jung's psychotherapy is a symbolic process that occurs within the context of a long term, one-to-one psychotherapeutic relationship. It is built on previous work. Similar to the alchemical myth, transformation has to begin with the *prima materia*, that is, a pile of despised, rejected, unwanted psychological material. It cannot be avoided. It is placed in a strong container that can withstand the heat of the affects from without and from within. The therapeutic relationship is that container. It is the crucible within which an alchemical transformation can occur (Jung 1946).

DIFFERENTIATED UNDERSTANDING OF THE EMOTIONS

There is a strong, self-protective reaction in us which seeks to deny emotions that overpower us. It is often difficult, as we know, to speak directly about some emotions. Sometimes we do not even know what we feel. A differentiated understanding of the emotions is of great value to both patient and psychotherapist. We can train ourselves to recognize the affects. One of the most useful approaches is through the study of the prototypical expressive actions of the fundamental emotions. The value of this to clinical practice is shown in the following example, when Jung recognized that hiding movements may express shame.

> CASE 4. A young lady, while guilelessly telling me a dream, for no apparent reason suddenly hid her face behind a curtain in an ostentatious manner. Analysis of the dream revealed a sexual wish which fully explained the reaction of shame.
>
> (Jung 1907, p. 47)

In addition to recognizing the expressive actions, it is of value to become familiar with the bodily innervations that are part of the affect. We may feel these as internal sensations, for example, the dry mouth of fear and the sick, nauseous feelings of humiliation.

I found it very exciting as I began to get more conscious of the typical patterns of the fundamental affects. But we do not have to re-invent the wheel. Darwin's classic study is a wonderful resource. Other more recent studies include the contributions of Tomkins, Eibl-Eibesfeldt, Ekman, Izard, and Stewart. The arts,

147

particularly dance and drama, also have much to teach us about the universal expressive actions of the emotions.

Another way to learn to recognize the affects is through observing infants and children. Infant observations ordinarily include a parent as well, so there is the opportunity to study the interaction of the parent and infant. However, a word of caution. It is important to be conscious of one's own material so that we do not project our own unconscious complexes on to the infants, children, or parents we are observing. This can be a problem for anyone, even the most prestigious of investigators. Melanie Klein, for example, whose great contribution to depth psychology was her advocacy of child analysis, became a victim of this tendency to see in others what is our own disposition. Lacking information about the prototypical expressive patterns of the innate emotions, she interpreted the infant's intense interest and excitement in feeding as greed. Greed is of course a complex family emotion that develops later in the child's life (Stewart in press).

In the early years of dance therapy, it was well understood that the movement preferences of the observer affect what the observer sees and reports. For example, an observer who moves with suddenness and quickness is likely to view others as if quickness were everyone's most natural attitude to time. Similarly, an observer who prefers a slow, sustained attitude to time, tends to view slowness as normal and everything faster as if it were acceleration. To get a balanced report of movement qualities, it is necessary to use at least three raters to observe the same movement event. The raters are chosen to represent as wide a range of movement preferences as possible (Clunis 1975, p. 33; Hunt 1964).

Just as dance therapy observers need to be aware of their movement preferences, observers of emotional expression need to be as aware as possible of their own complexes. In introductory courses in dance/movement as active imagination, one of the first topics explored is the tendency of the witness to project 'shadow' material (i.e. emotionally toned complexes of the personal unconscious) on to the mover. In the studio, the students form dyads. One is the mover, the other is the witness. After warming up together, the witnesses move back against a chair or wall, while the movers find a place for themselves, close their eyes and wait for an impulse to move. Each witness is attentive to his or her particular mover. But the initial task for the witness is to approach the mover as if s/he were a projective screen. When mover and witness come together afterwards to talk with each other, they expect that each will report a subjective experience. By beginning with the assumption that the experience of the witness is subjective, both mover and witness begin the gradual process of sorting out the feelings that are stirred as they work together. One of the ground rules in such a group is that each participant reflect on the experience and take a moment to consider what to say and what not to say. Part of the experience may want to be told – and part of it may want to be kept inside, contained. To support this sense of privacy, time is set aside also for journal writing, art materials and quiet reflection. The mover and witness relationship offers a valuable resource to the training of psychotherapists and analysts.

In psychotherapeutic practice, I have found it helpful to keep feelers out for the fourfold crisis emotions: Grief, Fear, Anger, Contempt/Shame. More often than not, three of the crisis affects are named; the bi-polar affect Contempt/Shame tends to be the missing fourth. In my experience, people frequently express their memories of grief, fear and anger, but then use a euphemistic term like 'hurt' or 'unsupported,' rather than speak directly of feeling shame. Another way of avoiding shame is to be so afraid of feeling it that we experience fear instead. For example, a person suffering from panic attacks realized that a large part of the underlying panic was fear of 'looking dumb.' With this realization came a flood of shameful memories and fantasies. As the terrible feelings could be felt and expressed directly, the frequency and intensity of the panic attacks began to subside. Shame may be the hardest emotion of all to let ourselves feel.

The images of pre-creation, the void, the abyss, chaos and alienation are the actual experiences of the innate crisis affects (Grief, Fear, Anger, Contempt/Shame). In clinical practice I have found awareness of these images to be particularly valuable when dissociation occurs. For example, the feeling of being 'on edge,' sometimes with my heart pounding, but without knowing what it is about – is typical of sitting on the edge of the abyss. If I let myself be with the image, I can begin to sense the terror of that bottomless pit. Another image is alienation. Whether witnessing dance/movement, or sitting in a chair across from a patient, I have sometimes felt as if I were a thousand miles away. Sometimes even our voices take on an alien quality, as if in an echo chamber. Such moments are so uncomfortable that it is hard to stay with them. But to the degree that the patient and I can bear it, it leads to consciousness of a realm that is non-human, alien. Mythic images may include outer space – or the desert as wilderness. In ancient tradition, the scapegoat is driven away from the community, banished. Two other pre-creation images are chaos and the void. Chaos is such a confused, disordered state that we may not even know when we are in it. Tense muscles are a clue – we hold tight to defend against the impulse to strike out, kick or bite. Imagining the full expression of such movements may help us begin to identify what is the matter and gradually get in touch with a more modulated, conscious expression of anger.

Finally, we come to the void. In an earlier chapter I described the dissociation of just going blank. If we can stay with the emptiness and begin to imagine around it, we may begin to feel it again. That hollow, vacant feeling inside and out is a reminder of what has been lost. With that connection, we can begin to move into and through the grief.

THE EXPERIENCE OF THE WITNESS

Although a wide range of feelings are involved, part of the witness is always fluctuating back and forth between curiosity and imagination. Curiosity is the essence of Logos or directed consciousness. Imagination is the essence of Eros or fantasy consciousness (Stewart 1986, pp. 190–4). In Chinese philosophy, these two interdependent modes are called Yang and Yin. Throughout human history they have been known by many names. The alchemists spoke of a mysterious marriage between Sol and Luna. Let us take a moment and imagine how the same landscape might be affected by sunlight and by moonlight. Sunlight, or a solar attitude, offers us clarity. It enables us to divide what we see into its separate parts. But when it gets too bright, everything becomes harsh, glaring and dry. When the sun is at its peak, we live in a world without shadow. The moon, on the other hand, reflects a mild light. It reveals a moist, shimmering landscape. Everything merges. In the darkness we find an unsuspected unity.

What does this have to do with witnessing movement? The witness fluctuates between a solar, differentiated, objective, definitive way of seeing, and a lunar, merging, subjective, imaginative way of seeing. The same movement event may be seen and described in many ways.

As I watch, I see the mover crouch low with her face hidden. Only her arms reach forward, with wide-spaced hands pressing flat on the ground. With an increasingly deep cycle of breathing, she slowly drops forward onto her knees and elbows, and finally slides flat onto her stomach, stretched full length on the ground. Her arms draw together in a long narrow shape, slipping between her body and the floor. She rests, breathing deeply.

As I watch, I let myself imagine and remember what it is like to go deeply inside. I know that this woman was largely ignored during the early years of her life, due to a series of illnesses in her family. As I watch, I feel an ache in my throat and my heart goes out to her. I now see her as if she were a very young infant. I imagine holding her close to my body, we rock back and forth with merging rhythms. As I imagine holding her and rocking her, I slowly become aware that I am actually rocking slightly. Later on, I realize that our breathing has become synchronous.

As she presses her hands into the ground, I experience mounting tension and for a moment, I'm fearful that she'll press harder and harder and suddenly explode. But instead, she slides forward and lies on her stomach. She has now withdrawn so much that there is very little movement. My mind wanders. I pick at a hangnail. I feel irritated with her, then guilty and irritated with myself. I imagine she is sitting on a volcano. In any case, it feels as if I am: my shoulder muscles are contracted, my jaw is tight, I'm not breathing very much. My mind dimly wonders whether I might be picking up something about her father's cycle of violent outbursts and subsequent remorse. Or is her withdrawal too close to my own way of avoiding anger?

As she kneels low, the shape of her body reminds me of the Moslem prayer ritual. Another image comes: one of the paintings Jung did for his Red Book shows a little figure that bows low, while covering its face. An enormous fire spout is erupting out of the earth in front of the little person. It fills the upper half of the painting with intricately formed red, orange, and yellow flames.

(Chodorow 1986, pp. 95–6)

After the sequence the mover's first words were: 'I feel as if I'm about to explode.' Then she sat up slowly, took a deep breath and began to tell me about the intense, pent up feelings.

In the narrative above I try to express something of the experience of witnessing. Even a little bit of movement goes a long way. There are many different levels of witnessing. On one level, you notice what the body is doing. What are the actual movements?

151

What parts of the body touch the ground? When the mover changes from one level to another, how does it happen? What are the patterns of tension? What are the body shapes and how do they change? How does breathing relate to the movement?

But at the same time, there is empathic relatedness, emotional attunement. If the mover is expressing an infantile quality, something of a parental, caregiving, nurturing feeling may come up in the witness. Or if the mover experienced early neglect or mistreatment, those kinds of indifferent, irritable or rejecting countertransference responses can also erupt. It is also possible that the witness stayed up too late the night before and feels irritable or indifferent for lack of sleep. Or it may be that the mover is approaching material that stirs up unconscious complexes in the witness. Naturally, when a strong emotional response comes up in the witness, it is essential to reflect as best we can on its source and meaning.

Then there is the whole realm of cultural association and amplification. From a larger cultural perspective, what does this person's movement bring to mind? How has this attitude or movement sequence appeared in art? How has it appeared in literature or mythology? What paintings come to mind? What kind of sculpture? What kind of poetry or music comes to mind as I watch the person move? The larger question here is how does the mover express a universal human experience?

It seems natural that we close with more questions than answers. The core of work with dance/movement in psychotherapy and analysis is the experience of the mover, the experience of the witness and the relationship between them that serves as container and process. The work is sustained by Jung's vision of individuation.

When the great swing has taken an individual into the world of symbolic mysteries, nothing comes of it, nothing can come of it, unless it has been associated with the earth, unless it has happened when that individual was in the body .... And so individuation can only take place if you first return to the body, to your earth, only then does it become true.

(Jung 1930–1934 vol. 2, p. 473)

APPENDIX: EMOTIONS AND THE UNIVERSAL GAMES

'The universal games constellate emotions or sets of emotions which are equilibrated through the process of playing the games' (Stewart 1987a, p. 37). When we look at the structure of the universal games, we find a fourfold categorization: games of *physical skill*, games of *chance*, games of *strategy* and *central person* games. Players have to bear, contain and ultimately transform such feelings as disappointment (physical skill), anxiety (chance), frustration (strategy), and embarrassment (central person). Naturally a wide range of affects and various emotional complexes will be constellated in different individuals as they play a game. But the modulated affects shown above are directly related to the structure and rules of each of the fourfold games.

Games of physical skill, chance, strategy and central person evoke the affective dynamisms: *rhythmic harmony, ritual, reason* and *relationship*, respectively. The dynamisms are modulations and transformations of the affects that are constellated in the playing of the games.

Games of physical skill foster the development of rhythmic harmony. But rhythmic harmony tends to come and go. We have it one moment and lose it the next. In the process of playing the game, we learn to bear our disappointment as we reach to catch, but miss the ball. The next time we may catch it. Those who enjoy playing games of physical skill usually have a good sensation function; such games are also related to the aesthetic attitude.

Games of chance foster the development of ritual. Whether we are children throwing dice, or adults spinning the wheel of fortune, the outcome of the game is in the hands of the Gods: we close our eyes, hold the dice (or roulette wheel) in a certain way, and whisper a short prayer to Lady Luck. If we win, we will try to remember every detail of what we did and how we did it – so we can do it the same way next time. By playing the game, we learn to contain, modulate and transform the fear that is constellated from this encounter with the unknown. Those who love to play games of chance seem to rely on their sense of intuition. There also seems to be an archaic link between games of chance and the religious attitude.

Games of strategy foster the development of reason. Whether checkers, chess, go or string figures, the outcome of the game is determined by the rational choices one makes. By playing the game, we learn to bear a sustained, intensely concentrated focus. Irritable impulses that come up tend to get channeled into the symbolic attack of the game. Those who like to play games of strategy are usually good thinkers, with the tendency toward a philosophic attitude.

Central person games foster relationship. Whether tag, hide and seek, musical chairs, or farmer in the dell, central person games designate one child at a time to be 'IT.' Whether we are IT for a few seconds or for a longer time, the game is played as an interaction between a central child and the group as a whole. The process involves the tension of not knowing how long we can stay in the game before we're 'out.' The winner is usually the last one – the one who has endured the tension for the longest time. Such games seem to deliberately evoke the experience of rejection. But the rules of the game are fair enough and the game is fun enough that such painful experiences can be tolerated – even integrated. Children who enjoy central person games seem to have a good beginning on the development of their feeling function, as well as a social attitude.

Many games have elements of more than one category. For example, football involves strategy as well as physical skill. But the oldest universal games tend to emphasize a single category, its related affective tone and expressive dynamism.

> The structure and rules of any commonly played game involve the deliberate evocation of one or more specific emotions which it may be suggested, are transformed in the playing of the game and explains why it has evolved in the form it has, and why it survives.
>
> (Stewart 1985, p. 93)

BIBLIOGRAPHY

Adler, J. (1973) Integrity of body and psyche: Some notes on work in process. *What is dance therapy, really?* eds. B. Govine and J. Chodorow, pp. 42–53. Columbia, Maryland: American Dance Therapy Association.

—— (1987) Who is the witness? *Contact Quarterly*, Winter 1987: 20–9.

Allan, J. (1988) *Inscapes of the child's world*. Dallas: Spring Publications.

Aristotle (n.d.) *The politics*, trans. T.A. Sinclair. Baltimore: Penguin Books, 1962.

Avstreith, A. (1981) The emerging self: Psychoanalytic concepts of self development and their implications for dance therapy. *American Journal of Dance Therapy*, 4/2: 21–32.

Axline, V. (1964) *Dibs in search of self*. New York: Ballantine Books, 1976.

Barasch, M. (1976) *Gestures of despair*. New York: New York University Press.

Bartenieff, I. (with D. Lewis) (1980) *Body movement: Coping with the environment*. New York: Gordon & Breach Science Publishers.

Beebe, J. (1987) Discussion: Original morality. *The archetype of shadow in a split world*, ed. M.A. Mattoon, pp. 84–9. Einsiedeln, Switzerland: Daimon Verlag.

Bernstein, P.L. (1984) *Theoretical approaches in dance-movement therapy*, volume II, Dubuque: Kendall/Hunt.

—— (1985) Embodied transformational images in dance-movement therapy. *Journal of Mental Imagery*, 9/4: 1–8.

Bernstein, P.L. and Singer, D.L. (1982) *The choreography of object relations*. Keene: Antioch New England Graduate School.

Blackmer, J.D. (1989) *Acrobats of the gods: Dance and transformation*. Toronto: Inner City Books.

Blom, L.A. and L.T. Chaplin (1988) *The moment of movement-dance improvisation*. Pittsburgh, PA: University of Pittsburgh Press.

Bolen, J.S. (1984) *Goddesses in everywoman*. New York: Harper & Row.

Bosanquet, C. (1970) Getting in touch. *Journal of Analytical Psychology*, 15/1: 42–58.

Bruch, H. (1974) *Learning psychotherapy, rationale and ground rules*. Cambridge, Massachusetts: Harvard University Press.

155

Caillois, R. (1958) *Man, play and games.* New York: Schocken Books, 1979.

Campbell, J. (1949) *The hero with a thousand faces.* New York: Bollingen Foundation, Meridian Edition, 1956.

—— (1959) *The masks of God: Primitive mythology.* New York: The Viking Press, Penguin Books, 1977.

Chace, M. (1953) Dance as an adjunctive therapy with hospitalized patients. *Bulletin of the Menninger Clinic,* 17: 219–55.

—— (1975) *Marian Chace: Her papers.* ed. H. Chaiklin. Columbia, Maryland: American Dance Therapy Association.

Chaiklin, S. (1975) Dance therapy. In *American handbook of psychiatry,* vol. 5, ed. S. Arieti, pp. 701–20. 2nd ed. New York: Basic Books.

Cheney, G. (1989) *Basic concepts in modern dance.* 3rd edition. Princeton: Princeton Book Company.

Chodorow, J. (1974) Philosophy and methods of individual work. In *Dance therapy: Focus on dance VII,* ed. K. Mason, pp. 24–6. Washington, D.C.: American Association for Health, Physical Education and Recreation.

—— (1977) Dance therapy and the transcendent function. *American Journal of Dance Therapy,* 2/1: 16–23, 1978.

—— (1982)Dance/movement and body experience in analysis. *Jungian analysis,* ed. M. Stein, pp. 192–203. La Salle: Open Court.

—— (1984) To move and be moved. *Quadrant* 17/2: 39–48.

—— (1986) The body as symbol: Dance/movement in analysis. *The body in analysis,* eds, N. Schwartz-Salant and M. Stein, pp. 87–108. Wilmette, Illinois: Chiron Publications.

—— (n.d.) unpublished notes

Clunis, D.M. (1975) *Expressive movement style affinities and personality characteristics.* Doctoral dissertation, University of California, Santa Barbara.

Dallett, J. (1982) Active imagination in practice. *Jungian analysis,* ed. M. Stein, pp. 173–91. La Salle: Open Court.

Daniels, J. (1974) *Dance-movement therapy.* Master's thesis, Goddard College, Vermont.

Darwin, C. (1872) *The expression of the emotions in man and animals.* Chicago and London: The University of Chicago Press, 1965, fifth impression, 1974.

Davidson, D. (1966) Transference as a form of active imagination. *Journal of Analytical Psychology,* 11/2: 135–46.

de Mille, A. (1951) *Dance to the piper.* Boston: Little, Brown and Company.

Dosamantes-Alperson, E. (1987) Transference and countertransference issues in movement psychotherapy. *The Arts in Psychotherapy,* 14: 209–14.

Dreifuss, G. (1987) Voice dialogue and holocaust. *The archetype of shadow in a split world,* ed. M.A. Mattoon, pp. 425–9. Einsiedeln, Switzerland: Daimon Verlag.

Edinger, E. (1974) *Ego and archetype.* Baltimore, Maryland: Penguin Books, Inc.

Eibl-Eibesfeldt, I. (1972) Similarities and differences between cultures in expressive movements. *Non-verbal communication*, ed. R.A. Hinde, pp. 297–314. London: Cambridge University Press, 1975.

Ekman, P., ed. (1972) *Emotion in the human face*, 2nd edition. Cambridge: Cambridge University Press.

—— (1984) Expression and the nature of emotion. *Approaches to emotion*, eds. K. Scherer and P. Ekman, pp. 319–43. Hillsdale, New Jersey: Lawrence Erlbaum.

—— (1989) The argument and evidence about universals in facial expressions of emotion. *Handbook of social psychophysiology*, eds. H. Wagner and A. Manstead, pp. 143–64. New York: John Wiley & Sons Ltd.

Eliade, M. (1963) *Myth and reality*. New York: Harper and Row, 1975.

—— (1967) *From primitives to Zen: A thematic sourcebook of the history of religions*. New York: Harper & Row, 1977.

Ellenberger, H.F. (1970) *The discovery of the unconscious*. New York: Basic Books.

Erikson, Erik H. (1963) *Childhood and society*. New York: W.W. Norton and Co., Inc.

Fay, C.G. (1977) *Movement and fantasy: A dance therapy model based on the psychology of C.G. Jung*. Master's Thesis, Goddard College, Vermont.

—— (1978) Five dance therapists whose life and work have been influenced by the psychology of C.G. Jung. *American Journal of Dance Therapy* 2/2: 17–18.

Frantz, G. (1972) An approach to the center: An interview with Mary Whitehouse. *Psychological Perspectives* 3: 37–46.

Franz, M.L. von. (1964) The process of individuation. *Man and his symbols*, eds. C.G. Jung and M.L. von Franz, pp. 158–229. New York: Doubleday & Company Inc.

—— (1978) *Interpretation of fairy tales*. Irving, Texas: Spring Publications.

Freud, S. (1900) *The interpretation of dreams*. New York: Basic Books, 1955.

Frisbie, C.J. (1967) *Kinaaldá: A study of the Navaho girl's puberty ceremony*. Wesleyan University Press.

Govine, B., C. Burton, J. Chodorow, D. Fletcher, G. Fox, A. Hawkins, S. Lovell, P. Van Pelt. (1973) Conceptual model. *What is dance therapy, really?*, eds. B. Govine and J. Chodorow, pp. 133–4. Columbia, Maryland: American Dance Therapy Association.

Graves, R. and R. Patai. (1963) *Hebrew myths: The book of Genesis*. New York: McGraw-Hill, 1966.

Greene, A. (1983) Giving the body its due. *Quadrant* 17/2: 9–24, 1984.

—— (1987) Book review of E. Gendlin's "Let your body interpret your dreams." *Quadrant* 20/1: 104–8.

Greenspan, S.I. and N.T. Greenspan. (1985) *First feelings*. New York: Viking Penguin Inc.

Gross, R.M. (1983) Steps toward feminine imagery of Deity in Jewish theology. *On being a Jewish feminist*, ed. S. Heschel, pp. 234–47. New York: Schocken Books.

Hall, J. (1977) *Clinical uses of dreams: Jungian interpretations and enactments*. New York: Grune & Stratton.

Hannah, B. (1953) Some remarks on active imagination. *Spring*, pp. 38–58.

—— (1981) *Active imagination*. Santa Monica: Sigo Press.

Hawkins, A. (1972) Work with patients. *Dance therapy: Roots and extensions*, ed. D. Cook, pp. 67–9. Columbia, Maryland: American Dance Therapy Association.

Hawkins A. and J. Chodorow, for the conference committee. (1980) Call for presentations for the 1980 National Conference. Photocopy. Columbia, Maryland: American Dance Therapy Association.

Haynes, S. (1984) *Authentic movement as one tool for redefining feminine identity in the Jungian active imagination process*. Doctoral dissertation, University of Massachusetts.

Henderson, J.L. (1962) The archetype of culture. *The archetype, proceedings of the 2nd international congress of Psychology, Zurich*. New York: S. Karger, 1964, pp. 3–15.

—— (1964) Ancient myths and modern man. *Man and his symbols*, eds. C.G. Jung and M.L. von Franz, pp. 104–57. New York: Doubleday & Company Inc.

—— (1967) *Thresholds of initiation*. Middletown, Connecticut: Wesleyan University Press.

—— (1977) Individual lives in a changing society. *Psychological Perspectives* 8/2: 126–42.

—— (1984) *Cultural attitudes in psychological perspective*. Toronto: Inner City Books.

—— (1985) The origins of a theory of cultural attitudes. *Psychological Perspectives* 16/2: 210–20.

—— (1985/1986) private conversation.

—— (n.d.) The cultural unconscious. Manuscript, pp. 1–22.

Hendricks, G. and K. Hendricks. (1983) *The moving center: Exploring movement activities for the classroom*. Englewood Cliffs, New Jersey: Prentice-Hall, Inc.

Hillman, J. (1961) *Emotion, A comprehensive phenomenology of theories and their meanings for therapy*. Evanston: Northwestern University Press.

—— (1976) *Suicide and the soul*. Zurich: Spring Publications.

—— (1983) Active imagination: The healing art. *Healing Fiction*, pp. 78–81. Barrytown, New York: Station Hill Press.

Hubback, J. (1988) *People who do things to each other: Essays in analytical psychology*. Wilmette, Illinois: Chiron Publications.

Humbert, E. (1971) Active imagination: Theory and practice. *Spring* 1971: 101–14.

Hunt, V. (1964) Movement behavior: A model for action. *Quest*, Monograph #2, pp. 69–91.

Izard, C.E. (1977) *Human emotions*. New York: Plenum Press.

Jung, C.G. (1902) On the psychology and pathology of so-called occult phenomena. *Collected works 1*, 1–88. Princeton: Princeton University Press, 1975.

—— (1907) The psychology of dementia praecox. *Collected works 3*, pp. 1–151. Princeton: Princeton University Press, 1972.

—— (1911) On the doctrine of complexes. *Collected works 2*,

pp. 598–604. Princeton: Princeton University Press, 1973.
—— (1912a) Two kinds of thinking. *Collected works 5*, pp. 7–33.
Princeton: Princeton University Press, 1967.
—— (1912b) The concept of libido. *Collected works 5*, pp. 132–41.
Princeton: Princeton University Press, 1967.
—— (1912c) The transformation of libido. *Collected works 5*, pp.
142–70. Princeton: Princeton University Press, 1967.
—— (1912/1928) On psychic energy. *Collected works 8*, pp. 3–66.
Princeton: Princeton University Press, 1975.
—— (1916) The transcendent function. *Collected works 8*, pp. 67–91.
Princeton: Princeton University Press, 1975.
—— (1917) (1917/1926/1943) On the psychology of the unconscious.
Collected works 7, pp. 1–119. Princeton: Princeton University Press,
1966.
—— (1919) Instinct and the unconscious. *Collected works 8*, pp. 129–38.
Princeton: Princeton University Press, 1975.
—— (1920) The psychological foundations of belief in spirits.
Collected works 8, pp. 300–18. Princeton: Princeton University
Press, 1975.
—— (1921) Psychological types. *Collected works 6*, Princeton:
Princeton University Press, 1977.
—— (1927) The structure of the psyche. *Collected works 8*, pp. 139–58.
Princeton: Princeton University Press, 1975.
—— (1928a) The relations between the ego and the unconscious.
Collected works 7, pp. 121–241. Princeton: Princeton University
Press, 1966.
—— (1928b) The spiritual problem of modern man. *Collected works
10*, pp. 74–94. 2nd ed. Princeton: Princeton University Press, 1970
—— (1929) Commentary on 'The secret of the golden flower'.
Collected works 13, pp. 1–56. Princeton: Princeton University Press,
1976.
—— (1930s) *Zarathustra Seminars*, Volume One, unpublished.
—— (1930–34) *The Visions Seminars*. From the complete notes of Mary
Foote, Books One and Two. Zurich: Spring Publications, 1976.
—— (1931a) The aims of psychotherapy. *Collected works 16*, pp. 36–52.
Princeton: Princeton University Press, 1975.
—— (1931b) Problems of modern psychotherapy. *Collected works 16*,
pp. 53–75. Princeton: Princeton University Press, 1975.
—— (1933) Brother Klaus. *Collected works 11*, pp. 316–23. Princeton:
Princeton University Press, 1975.
—— (1934a) A review of the complex theory. *Collected works 8*, pp.
92–104. Princeton: Princeton University Press, 1975.
—— (1934b) A study in the process of individuation. *Collected works
9/1*, pp. 290–354. Princeton: Princeton University Press, 1977.
—— (1935) The Tavistock lectures: On the theory and practice of
analytical psychology. *Collected works 18*, pp. 5–182. Princeton:
Princeton University Press, 1976.
—— (1936a) Individual dream symbolism in relation to alchemy.
Collected works 12, pp. 41–223. Princeton: Princeton University
Press, 1974.

—— (1936b) The concept of the collective unconscious. *Collected works 9/1*, pp. 42–53. Princeton: Princeton University Press, 1977.

—— (1936c) Yoga and the West. *Collected works 11*, pp. 529–37. Princeton: Princeton University Press, 1975.

—— (1938a) Psychological aspects of the mother archetype. *Collected works 9, part I*, pp. 75–110. Princeton: Princeton University Press, 2nd edition, 1968.

—— (1938b) *Dream analysis*, ed. W. McGuire. Princeton: Princeton University Press, 1984.

—— (1940) The psychology of the child archetype. *Collected works, 9/1*, pp. 151–81. Princeton: Princeton University Press, 1977.

—— (1945) The phenomenology of the spirit in fairytales. *Collected works 9/1*, pp. 207–54. Princeton: Princeton University Press, 1977.

—— (1946) The psychology of the transference. *Collected works 16*, pp. 163–323. Princeton: Princeton University Press, 1975.

—— (1947) On the nature of the psyche. *Collected works 8*, pp. 159–234. Princeton: Princeton University Press, 1975.

—— (1951) Aion: Researches into the phenomenology of the Self. *Collected works 9, part II*. Princeton: Princeton University Press, 1968.

—— (1961a) *Memories, dreams, reflections*. New York: Random House – Vintage Books, 1965.

—— (1961b) Symbols and the interpretation of dreams. *Collected works 18*, pp. 185–266. Princeton: Princeton University Press, 1976.

—— (1963) *Mysterium coniunctionis*. Princeton: Princeton University Press, 1974.

—— (1973) *Letters*. Vol. 1. Princeton: Princeton University Press.

—— (1975) *Letters*. Vol. 2. Princeton: Princeton University Press.

Kalff, D. (1962) The archetype as a healing factor. *The archetype, Proceedings of the 2nd international congress of Analytical Psychology, Zurich*, pp. 182–200. Basel/New York: S. Karger, 1964.

—— (1971) Experiences with far eastern philosophers. *The analytic process*, ed. J.B. Wheelwright, pp. 56–67. New York: Putnam.

—— (1980) *Sandplay*. Santa Monica: Sigo Press.

Kollwitz, K. (1988) *The diary and letters of Kaethe Kollwitz*, ed. H. Kollwitz. Evanston, Illinois: Northwestern University Press.

Laban, R. (1971) *The mastery of movement*. Third edition. London: MacDonald & Evans.

Levy, F. (1988) *Dance movement therapy—a healing art*. Reston, Virginia: National Dance Association, AAHPERD.

Lockhart, R. (1983) *Words as eggs*. Dallas: Spring Publications.

Lopez-Pedraza, R. (1977) *Hermes and his children*. Zurich: Spring Publications.

Lynd, H. (1958) *On shame and the search for identity*. New York: Harcourt, Brace.

Machtiger, H.G. (1984) Reactions on the transference and countertransference process with borderline patients. *Chiron 1984*, pp. 101–29, eds. N. Schwartz-Salant and M. Stein.

McNeely, D.A. (1987) *Touching: Body therapy and depth psychology*. Toronto: Inner City Books.

Mindell, A. (1982) *Dreambody*. Los Angeles: Sigo Press.
—— (1985) *Working with the dreambody*. Boston: Routledge & Kegan Paul.
Nathanson, D.L., ed. (1987) *The many faces of shame*. New York: The Guilford Press.
Neumann, E. (1954) The separation of the world parents: The principle of opposites. In *The origins and history of consciousness*, pp. 102–27. Princeton: Princeton University Press, 1973.
—— (1966) Narcissism, normal self-formation, and the primary relation to the mother. *Spring 1966*, pp. 81–106.
—— (1973) *The child*. Boston: Shambala Publications, 1990.
Oppikofer, R. (1976/77) *A journey to 'my land.'* Master's thesis, Goddard College, Vermont.
Osterman, E. (1965) The tendency toward patterning and order in matter and in the psyche. *The reality of the psyche*, ed. J.B. Wheelwright, pp. 14–27. New York: G.P. Putnam's Sons, 1968.
Otto, Rudolf. (1923) *The idea of the holy*. Oxford/New York: Oxford University Press, 1981.
Perera, S.B. (1981) *Descent to the Goddess*. Toronto: Inner City Books.
—— (1986) *The scapegoat complex: Toward a mythology of shadow and guilt*. Toronto: Inner City Books.
Piaget, J. (1952) *The origins of intelligence in children*. New York: W.W. Norton & Co., Inc., 1963.
—— (1954) *The construction of reality in the child*. New York: Basic Books, Inc., 1971.
—— (1962) *Play, dreams and imitation in childhood*. New York: W.W. Norton & Co., Inc.
Proust, M. (1928) *The past recaptured*. New York: Random House, 1932 and renewed 1959.
Quintero, N. (1980) Coming of age. *National Geographic*, 157/2: 262–71.
Robbins, A., with contributors. (1980) *Expressive therapy*. New York: Human Sciences Press.
Roberts, J. and B. Sutton-Smith. (1970) The cross-cultural and psychological study of games. *The cross-cultural analysis of games*, ed. G. Luschen, pp. 100–8. Champaign, Illinois: Stipes.
Rossi, E.L. (1986) *The psychobiology of mind-body healing*. New York: W.W. Norton & Co., Inc.
Rutter, P. (1989) *Sex in the forbidden zone: When men in power – therapists, doctors, clergy, teachers, and others – betray women's trust*. Los Angeles: Jeremy P. Tarcher, Inc.
Sachs, C. (1937) *World history of the dance*. New York: Norton & Co.
Samuels, A. (1985) *Jung and the post-Jungians*. London and New York: Routledge & Kegan Paul.
—— (1987) Original morality in a depressed culture. *The archetype of shadow in a split world*, ed. M.A. Mattoon, pp. 69–83. Einsiedeln, Switzerland: Daimon Verlag.
—— 1989. *The plural psyche*. London and New York: Routledge.
Samuels, A., B. Shorter and F. Plaut. (1986) *A critical dictionary of Jungian analysis*. London: Routledge & Kegan Paul.

Sandner, D. (1979) *Navaho symbols of healing*. New York: Harcourt, Brace, Jovanovich, Inc.

Schaya, L. (1971) *The universal meaning of the Kaballah*. Baltimore: Penguin Books, Inc., 1973.

Schmais, C. (1974) Dance therapy in perspective. *Dance therapy: Focus on dance VII*, ed. K. Mason, pp. 7–12. Washington D.C.: American Association for Health, Physical Education and Recreation.

Schoop, T. (with P. Mitchell). (1974) *Won't you join the dance?* Palo Alto: National Press Books.

—— (1983) Comments in response to "A Tribute to Trudi Schoop. " Presented at the 18th Annual Conference of the American Dance Therapy Association. Asilomar, California: October 1983.

Schwartz-Salant, N. (1982) *Narcissism and character transformation*. Toronto: Inner City Books.

—— (1984) Review of Jungian analysis. *The San Francisco Institute Library Journal*, 5/2: 14–27.

Siegel, E. (1984) *Dance-movement therapy: Mirror of ourselves*. New York: Human Sciences Press.

Singer, J. (1972) *Boundaries of the soul*. Garden City, New York: Doubleday & Co., Inc.

—— (1976) *Androgyny*. Garden City, N.Y.: Anchor Press/Doubleday.

Stein, M. (1983) Power, shamanism, and maieutics in the counter-transference. *Chiron 1984*, eds. N. Schwartz-Salant and M. Stein.

Stern, D.N. (1985) *The interpersonal world of the infant*. New York: Basic Books, Inc.

Stevens, A. (1983) *Archetypes: A natural history of the self*. New York: Quill.

Stewart, C.T. (1981) Developmental psychology of sandplay. *Sandplay studies: Origins, theory and practice*, ed. G. Hill, pp. 39–92. San Francisco: C.G. Jung Institute of San Francisco.

Stewart, C.T. and Stewart, L.H. (1981) Play, games and stages of development: A contribution toward a comprehensive theory of play. Presented at the 7th annual conference of The Association for the Anthropological Study of Play (TAASP). Fort Worth, April 1981.

Stewart, L.H. (1976) Kinship libido: Toward an archetype of the family. *Proceedings of the Annual conference of Jungian analysts of the United States*, pp. 168–82. San Francisco: C.G. Jung Institute of San Francisco.

—— (1977) Sand Play therapy: Jungian technique. *International encyclopedia of psychiatry, psychology, psychoanalysis and neurology*, ed. B. Wolman, pp. 9–11. New York: Aesculapius Publishers.

—— (1978) Gaston Bachelard and the poetics of reverie. *The shaman from Elko*, ed. G. Hill, *et al.* San Francisco: C.G. Jung Institute of San Francisco.

—— (1981a) Play and sandplay. *Sandplay studies: Origins, theory and practice*, ed. G. Hill, pp. 21–37. San Francisco: C.G. Jung Institute of San Francisco.

—— (1981b) The play-dream continuum and the categories of the imagination. Presented at the 7th annual conference of the

Association for the Anthropological Study of Play. Fort Worth: April 1981.

—— (1982) Sandplay and analysis. *Jungian analysis*, ed. M. Stein, pp. 204–18. La Salle: Open Court Publishing Co.

—— (1984) Play-eros, in Affects and archetypes II. Paper presented at active imagination seminar in Geneva, Switzerland in August 1984.

—— (1985) Affect and archetype: A contribution to a comprehensive theory of the structure of the psyche. In the *Proceedings of the 1985 California Spring Conference*, pp. 89–120. San Francisco: C.G. Jung Institute.

—— (1986) Work in progress: Affect and archetype. *The body in analysis*, eds. N. Schwartz-Salant and M. Stein, pp. 183–203. Wilmette, Illinois: Chiron Publications.

—— (1987a) A brief report: Affect and archetype. *Journal of Analytical Psychology* 32/1: 35–46.

—— (1987b) Affect and archetype in analysis. *Archetypal processes in psychotherapy*, eds. N. Schwartz-Salant and M. Stein, pp. 131–62. Wilmette, Illinois: Chiron Publications.

—— (1987c) private conversation

—— (1987d) Kinship libido: Shadow in marriage and family. *The archetype of shadow in a split world*, ed. M.A. Mattoon, pp. 387–99. Einsiedeln, Switzerland: Daimon Verlag.

—— (1990) Foreword, in new edition of E. Neumann's *The child*. Boston: Shambhala Publications.

—— (in press) Jealousy and envy: Complex family emotions. *The family: Personal, cultural and archetypal dimensions*, eds. L.H. Stewart and J. Chodorow. Boston: Sigo Press.

Stewart, L.H. and Stewart, C.T. (1979) Play, games and affects: A contribution toward a comprehensive theory of play. In Play as context, ed. A.T. Cheska, pp. 42–52. *Proceedings of The Association for the Anthropological Study of Play* (TAASP). Westpoint, N.Y.: Leisure Press, 1981.

Sullwold, E. (1971) Eagle eye. *The well tended tree*, ed. H. Kirsch, pp. 235–52. New York: Putnam.

Sutton-Smith, B. (1975) Play as adaptive potentiation. *Sportwissenschaft* 5: 103–18.

—— (1978) *The dialectics of play*. Schorndorf, West Germany: Verlag Karl Hofman.

Tomkins, S. (1962) *Affect imagery consciousness*, Volume I. New York: Springer Publishing Company, Inc.

—— (1963) *Affect imagery consciousness*, Volume II. New York: Springer Publishing Company, Inc.

—— (1982) Affect theory. *Emotion in the human face*, 2nd edition, ed. P. Ekman, pp. 353–95. Cambridge: Cambridge University Press.

Ulanov, A. (1982) Transference/countertransference. *Jungian analysis*, ed. M. Stein, pp. 68–85. La Salle, Illinois, and London: Open Court.

Van der Post, L. (1979) World unrest as a loss of meaning. C.G. Jung Cassette Library. Los Angeles Jung Institute.

Watkins, M. (1976) *Waking dreams*. New York: Harper & Row, 1977.
Weiss, U. (1982) *Movement and dance therapy: My personal quest.* Unpublished manuscript.
Whitehouse, M. (1958) The Tao of the body. Paper presented at the Analytical Psychology Club of Los Angeles.
—— (1963) Physical movement and personality. Paper presented at the Analytical Psychology Club of Los Angeles, 1963.
—— (1968a) Reflections on a metamorphosis. *A well of living waters – Festschrift for Hilda Kirsch*, ed. R. Head, *et al.*, pp. 272–7. Los Angeles: C.G. Jung Institute, 1977.
—— (1968b) Introduction of videotape: Individual dance and verbal therapy session. *Workshop in dance therapy: Its research potentials*, ed. B. Bird, pp. 20–2. New York: Committee on research in dance.
—— (1977) The transference and dance therapy. *American Journal of Dance Therapy* 1/1: 3–7.
—— (1978) Conversation with Mary Whitehouse and Frieda Sherman. *American Journal of Dance Therapy* 2/2: 3–4.
—— (1979) C.G. Jung and dance therapy. *Eight theoretical approaches in dance-movement therapy*, ed. P.L. Bernstein, pp. 51–70. Dubuque: Kendall/Hunt.
—— (forthcoming) *The moving self: Dance to dance therapy.*
—— (n.d.) Creative expression in physical movement is language without words. Unpublished manuscript.
—— (n.d.) Some thoughts on movement, dance and the integration of the personality. Unpublished notes.
Whitmont, E. (1972) Body experience and psychological awareness. *Quadrant* 12: 5–16.
Winnicott, D.W. (1975) *Through paediatrics to psycho-analysis*. New York: Basic Books.
—— (1977) *The Piggle: An account of the psychoanalytic treatment of a little girl*. Ed. I. Ramzy. New York: International Universities Press, Inc., 1979.
Woodman, M. (1980) *The owl was a baker's daughter*. Toronto: Inner City Books.
—— (1982) *Addiction to perfection*. Toronto: Inner City Books.
—— (1983) Psyche/soma awareness. *Quadrant* 17/2: 25–37.
Wyman, W. (1978) *Merging and differentiating: A concept basic to growth and therapeutic process*. Master's thesis in dance, University of California at Los Angeles.
Young, E. (1965) *The nursery school program for culturally different children*. Menlo Park: Pacific Coast Publishers.
Zenoff, N. (1986) *The mother's experience after the sudden death of a child: Personal and transpersonal perspectives*. Doctoral dissertation, Institute of Transpersonal Psychology, Menlo Park, California.
—— (1986) An interview with Joan Chodorow. *American Journal of Dance Therapy*, 9: 6–22.

NAME INDEX

SUBJECT INDEX

abyss 83, 84, 89, 93, 95, 134, 149
action 68, 70
active imagination 1–2, 24, 27, 34, 51,
   60, 61, 72, 75, 102, 104, 106, 111,
   112, 113–16, 125; theoretical
   framework for 41; transformative
   function of 75; see also dance; play
admiration 78, 123
aesthetic attitude 53, 86, 87, 89, 93,
   95, 153
affective dynamisms 153
affects see emotions
aggression 69
alienation 83, 84, 91, 93, 95, 134, 149;
   from body 112
ambition 65
analysand 113
analysis see Jungian analysis;
   psychoanalysis
analyst 113, 140, 149
analytic process 29, 112
analytical: method 34; practice 111;
   psychology 2, 55, 71
anger 3, 5, 22, 62, 63, 64, 68, 69, 76,
   77, 81, 83, 84, 87, 89, 90, 91, 92,
   95, 121, 123, 149, 150; see also
   irritation; frustration; rage
anguish 77, 82, 125, 130; see also grief
anima and animus 55, 57–8, 79
anxiety 4, 67, 78, 153; see also fear
apperceptive aspect 88, 89, 90, 91
apprehension 4, 77; see also fear
archetypal: affects see emotion,
   archetypal; experience 46
art 87, 93, 112; diagnostic value of 34;
   therapeutic value of 34
attack 90
authentic: movement see movement,
   authentic; response 33
autism, in children 13

avarice 65

ballet exercises 34
Bartenieff Fundamentals 31
becoming 93
being 93
bodily innervations 4, 147
body: awareness 33, 60; -psyche
   relationship 41, 42, 43, 44, 144
breathing 34, 152

cathartic release 33, 34, 37, 75, 130,
   134
centering, affect of 65, 76, 77, 81, 84, 87
centroversion 97
Changing Woman 140
chaos 83, 84, 89, 90, 93, 95, 125, 134,
   149, 150
child development 13, 72, 96–101;
   within family 42, 66, 72, 78
cognition 70
collective unconscious see unconscious
compassion 78, 123
complex see emotional complex
complexio oppositorum 92, 93
compulsive actions 23
conceit 65
confession 144
conflict see emotional conflict
conscious: attitude 51; awareness 19,
   25, 28, 34, 36
consciousness 94; availability of
   unconscious to 54; development of
   42, 70, 76; differentiation of 100;
   directed 150; ego 53, 59; emotion
   as a source of 47, 76; fantasy in
   150; meeting with unconscious
   115; mythic 72; physical 37;
   self-reflective 59, 87, 112; stages of
   developing 139

167